AI FOR CHEMICAL INDUSTRY

BY

A B KHARE

BlueRose ONE.com
Stories Matter
NewDelhi • London

BLUEROSE PUBLISHERS
India | U.K.

BlueRose ONE.com
Stories Matter
NewDelhi • London

For permissions requests or inquiries regarding this publication,
please contact:

BLUEROSE PUBLISHERS
www.BlueRoseONE.com
info@bluerosepublishers.com
+91 8882 898 898
+4407342408967

ISBN: 978-93-7542-647-9

Cover design: A B Khare
Typesetting: Tanya Raj Upadhyay

First Edition: February 2026

Preface

About Author: A B Khare is a Chemical Engineer graduated from University of Roorkee now IIT Roorkee and have 45 years of experience in Chemical Industry and experience range from Management Trainee to working in shift, then head operation, plant Manager, Technical Services, Project Execution, Procurement Chief of Organization and then finally to Chairman and Managing Director of Two Listed Central Government of India Public Sector Companies and after retirement currently a Director of Listed, Chemical Public limited Company, beside this he was also director of three other Chemical companies. Any feedback or suggestion can be given by email to abkhare@hotmail.com or on whatsApp no 9869467771.

About Book: AI is no longer optional — it is essential for competitiveness and sustainability in the chemical sector. The chemical industry stands at the cusp of a technological revolution driven by Artificial Intelligence (AI). This book explores the intersection of AI and chemical Engineering, providing industry professionals with insights, case studies, and practical implementation strategies. Whether you are a chemical engineer, data scientist, or business leader, the chapters that follow will guide you through the applications, Implementation Strategies, benefits, and challenges of AI adoption and Future in the chemical sector. Whole book is having 25 Chapters and is divided into four Parts. Chapter covered into Part one, speaks about Core AI and Chemical Industry Foundations. Part Two Chapter describes AI in chemical Industry core Plant Operation. Part Three deals with AI in Business Functions of Chemical Industry. Part four described AI integration strategies in Chemical Industry and how to implement AI in different departments along with AI Future in Chemical Industry.

Table of Contents

Part one

Core AI & Chemical Industry Foundation

Chapter 1 – Introduction to AI and the Chemical Industry

1.1 Overview

The chemical industry is one of the world's most vital sectors, producing materials that underpin modern life—from pharmaceuticals and fertilizers to advanced polymers and specialty chemicals. It is also an industry characterized by complex processes, high capital intensity, and stringent safety and environmental regulations. In this challenging environment, Artificial Intelligence (AI) has emerged as a transformative force, capable of reshaping research, production, and business models.

While automation and process control systems have long been part of chemical plants, AI represents a leap forward. Unlike conventional control systems that rely on predefined rules, AI systems learn from data, adapt to changing conditions, and generate insights that can exceed human intuition. This evolution holds the potential to deliver step-change improvements in efficiency, quality, sustainability, and profitability, energy consumption, raw material consumption.

1.2 History and Evolution of Artificial Intelligence and Its Journey into the Manufacturing Industry

Artificial Intelligence (AI) has evolved from theoretical concepts into one of the most transformative technologies in modern history. Its impact spans across industries, with manufacturing being one of the biggest beneficiaries. This section provides a history of AI, the evolution of machine learning, deep learning, Large Language Models (LLMs), prompt engineering, AI agents, AI tools, and how these technologies reshaped manufacturing.

1. Early Foundations of AI (1940s–1950s)

- Alan Turing proposed the Turing Test in 1950.
- Early AI research explored logic, reasoning, and symbolic problem-solving.
- First computer programs simulated puzzles, mathematics, and decision-making.

3. Birth of AI as a Field (1956–1970s)

- 1956 Dartmouth Conference marked the formal beginning of AI.
- Symbolic AI and rule-based systems dominated research.
- Robotics research started; early automation concepts appeared.

4. AI Winters and Renewed Interest (1970s–1990s)

- Funding decreased due to unrealistic expectations.
- Expert systems revived AI in the 1980s.
- Another decline followed when systems became costly and difficult to maintain.

5. Rise of Machine Learning (1990s–2010)

- Transition from rule-based AI to statistical and data-based learning.
- Neural networks, decision trees, SVMs gained popularity.
- Early industrial adoption: predictive maintenance, quality analysis, forecasting.

6. Deep Learning Revolution (2010–Present)

- GPUs enabled large-scale neural networks.
- Breakthroughs in computer vision, natural language processing, and robotics.
- Manufacturing applications expanded: defect detection, automation, simulations.

7. Evolution of Large Language Models (LLMs)

- LLMs use transformer architecture (introduced in 2017).
- Key milestones:
    - Word2Vec (2013): vector embeddings
    - BERT (2018): contextual understanding
    - GPT (2018–present): generative reasoning, multi-step tasks
- Capabilities:
    - Natural language tasks
    - Technical documentation
    - Programming and automation
    - Knowledge extraction and reasoning
    - Enterprise workflow integration

LLM look like search engine but they are different as search response to search existing document or existing database, while LLM goes beyond existing knowledge and can do reasoning and understand the things and then give response.

8. Prompt Engineering

- Designing high-quality prompts to optimize LLM outputs.
- Techniques:
    - Zero-shot and few-shot prompting
    - Chain-of-thought prompting
    - Role-based prompting
    - Instruction-based prompting
- Uses in manufacturing:
    - SOP generation
    - Technical troubleshooting
    - Root-cause analysis
    - Process documentation
    - AI-powered control room support

9. AI Agents

- Autonomous systems able to:
    - Observe
    - Reason
    - Plan
    - Act
    - Improve with feedback
- AI agents can integrate with tools, APIs, databases, and company systems.
- Manufacturing applications:
    - Predictive maintenance agents
    - Real-time optimization agents
    - Scheduling and logistics agents
    - Digital twin orchestrators
    - Autonomous inspection & reporting agents

10. AI Tools and Ecosystem

- Key categories:
    - LLM tools (ChatGPT, Claude, Gemini)
    - Vision systems for automated QC
    - Robotics and cobots
    - IoT platforms and sensors
    - Simulation environments and digital twins
    - Workflow automation systems
- Benefits:
    - Speed
    - Scalability
    - Accuracy
    - Autonomous decision-making

11. AI's Journey into the Manufacturing Industry

- From basic automation to Industry 4.0 and now Industry 5.0.

- Milestones:
    - Automation (1970–1990)
    - Robotics and lean operations (1990–2010)
    - IoT-enabled smart factories (2010–2018)
    - AI-powered autonomous plants (2018–present)

12. Modern Manufacturing Applications

- Predictive maintenance using ML.
- AI-based process optimization.
- Vision-based quality inspection.
- Supply chain and logistics optimization.
- Autonomous robots and cobots.
- Energy efficiency optimization.
- Knowledge automation using LLMs.
- Safety and environmental monitoring.

1.3 Defining AI in the Context of the Chemical Industry

In its broadest sense, AI refers to computer systems designed to perform tasks that normally require human intelligence—such as learning, reasoning, decision-making, and perception.

In the chemical industry, AI's applications are often tied to:

Machine Learning (ML): Identifying patterns in historical and real-time process data to optimize operations or predict outcomes.

Computer Vision: Detecting quality deviations, leaks, or anomalies through automated visual inspection.

Natural Language Processing (NLP): Extracting insights from technical literature, regulatory texts, or safety documentation.

Optimization Algorithms: Fine-tuning reaction conditions, production schedules, or logistics in ways that balance cost, safety, and quality.

1.4 Why AI Matters Now

The convergence of four major trends is accelerating AI adoption in the chemical sector:

Data Availability

Modern plants generate terabytes of process data generated real time data for several hundreds or thousands parameters in bigger plants, quality data are generated online as well as through lab analysis, and maintenance data are also generated through on line sensors and one time sensors, Data generated through SAP or other plant management system, SCADA systems, and laboratory analysis are generated to judge quality of materials or for process analysis to generation plant conditions. These lab data are integrated as Lab information management systems (LIMS).

Computing Power

Cloud computing and high-performance GPUs have made it feasible to train complex AI models quickly and cost-effectively. Earlier these computing powers were used for plant control and optimization of process parameters.

Advanced Algorithms

Deep learning, reinforcement learning, and hybrid AI-physics models can now tackle the non-linear complexities of chemical reactions and process control.

Competitive Pressure

As cost of computing and software go down considerably in conjugation with rising energy costs, tighter environmental regulations, and global competition are pushing companies to seek smarter, more agile solutions.

1.5 Key Value Propositions of AI in the Chemical Industry

Process Optimization: Maximizing yield while reducing raw material and energy consumption in plant using complex model has become new normal.

Predictive Maintenance: From breakdown maintenance plant maintenance has moved to planned maintenance to predictive maintenance, This Prevent unplanned downtime by forecasting equipment failures before they occur and take proper action to minimize its effect on plant efficiency.

Faster R&D Cycles: pharma Industry has accelerating new material discovery reducing time for discovering new drugs and formulation through AI-assisted simulations.

Enhanced Safety: Predicting hazards, improving emergency response, and reducing human exposure to dangerous conditions.

Sustainability Gains: Reducing waste and emissions through precise control and optimization.

1.6 Barriers and Challenges

AI adoption in the chemical industry is not without obstacles:

Data Silos and data quality Issues: Inconsistent data formats and incomplete historical records hinder model accuracy. Even inconsistency of data quality pose big challenges in model perfection of process control and process optimization.

Change Management: Resistance from workforce segments unfamiliar with AI technologies.

Integration with Legacy Systems: Many plants operate with decades-old control systems not designed for AI connectivity. Which are very difficult to modernize due to very high cost and even some time not possible due high plant downtime. This is due to the fact that losses associated with long shutdown required for modernization most of the time out weigh the gain arising by implementing AI integration.

Regulatory Concerns: The need to ensure AI-driven decisions comply with industry standards and legal requirements.

1.7 The Road Ahead

AI is not a silver bullet, but rather a strategic enabler. Companies that treat AI as a core capability—integrating it into R&D, operations, and business planning—will be positioned to achieve sustained competitive advantage.

In the chapters ahead, we will explore in detail how AI technologies can be deployed across the chemical value chain, illustrated by case studies, adoption frameworks, and best practices.

Key Takeaway:

AI in the chemical industry is moving from an experimental concept to a competitive necessity. Its successful implementation requires not just technology investment, but also cultural change, robust data governance, and alignment with strategic goals. AI has transformed from mathematical theories to a powerful industrial force. With LLMs, AI agents, digital twins, and advanced automation, the manufacturing world is entering an era of intelligent, efficient, and autonomous operations.

Chapter 2 – The Chemical Industry Landscape

The chemical industry is one of the world's most diverse, complex, and strategically important sectors. It underpins countless other industries—energy, agriculture, manufacturing, healthcare, construction, electronics—yet often operates behind the scenes. Understanding the landscape of this industry is essential before exploring how artificial intelligence (AI) can create meaningful transformation.

2.1 Structure of the Chemical Industry

The industry can be broadly divided into three main segments:

Commodity Chemicals

These include basic chemicals such as Fertilizers, Petrochemicals, ethylene, propylene, methanol, ammonia, Urea, Sulfuric acid.

Characteristics: They have high production volumes, price-sensitive markets, and tight profit margins.

AI Relevance: Process optimization, energy efficiency, and predictive maintenance.

Specialty Chemicals

Products tailored for specific applications—paints, coatings, adhesives, catalysts, and additives.

Characteristics: Lower volumes, higher margins, and greater technical differentiation.

AI Relevance: Formulation design, quality control, and rapid product development.

Fine and Life Science Chemicals

Highly complex, small-volume chemicals such as pharmaceuticals, agrochemicals, and flavors/fragrances.

Characteristics: High R&D intensity, stringent regulatory requirements.

AI Relevance: Accelerated molecule discovery, regulatory text analysis, and clinical data mining.

2.2 Key Operational Challenges

AI's transformative potential becomes clearer when we examine the industry's persistent challenges:

Energy Intensity: Many processes consume massive amounts of heat and power. Even a 1–2% efficiency gain can save millions annually.

Complex Process Dynamics: Multivariable reactions and interdependent process parameters interactions are highly non-linear. Which make optimization challenging without advanced analytics.

Quality Consistency: Small variations in raw material quality or environmental conditions can cause product defects.

Maintenance & Downtime: Unplanned shutdowns can cause large production and revenue losses.

Safety & Compliance: Hazardous materials and strict environmental regulations require constant monitoring and documentation.

Market Volatility: Price swings in feedstocks and fluctuating global demand require agile supply chain strategies.

2.3 The Digital Transformation Push

While automation and process control have been part of chemical plants for decades, the industry is now entering a new phase of digital transformation. The difference today is the integration of real-time data, advanced analytics, and AI into decision-making at all levels:

From Lab to Plant: AI can bridge the gap between R&D data and large-scale manufacturing parameters.

From Plant to Market: Predictive analytics can align production schedules with dynamic market demand and product prices.

From Reactive to Proactive: Maintenance, safety, and quality are increasingly managed through prediction rather than response.

2.4 Why AI Is a Natural Fit

Chemical processes are data-rich but insight-poor. Every plant generates vast amounts of information from:

- Distributed Control Systems (DCS)
- Laboratory Information Management Systems (LIMS)
- Quality control sensors
- Online machinery health data like Bearing temperature and machine vibration.
- Supply chain ERP systems

Historically, much of this data has been underutilized. AI can turn these vast datasets into actionable intelligence, enabling:

- Process optimization at scale
- Better Predictive Maintenance.
- Faster R&D cycles
- Improved safety and environmental performance
- Better market responsiveness

2.5 Structure of Chemical Industry

Typical Material flow Diagram of Fertilizer plants is given bellow.

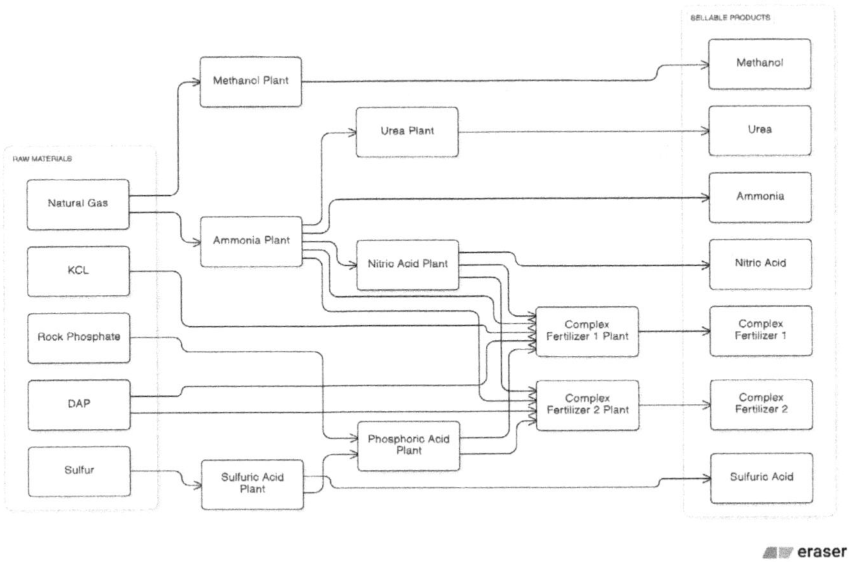

Departmental Diagram of Chemical Company

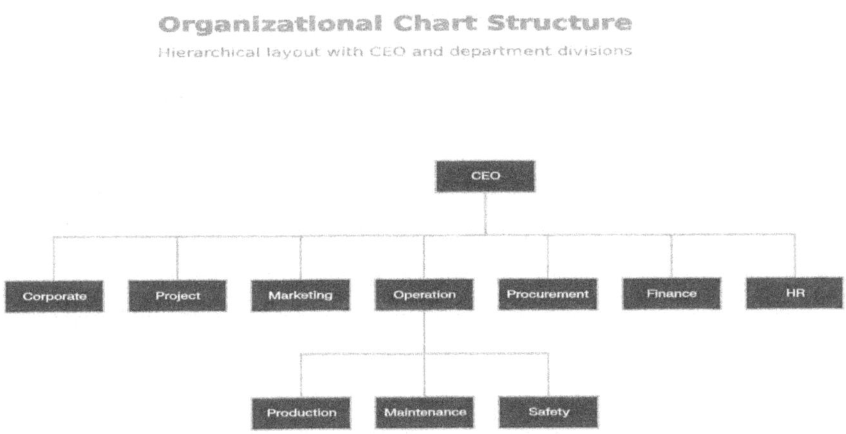

Each chemical company carryout different type of activities. They are mainly

For Expansion

- Project Conceiving
- Project Execution for new plants.

For Existing Plant Operation

- Raw material procurement
- Operation or processing of Chemicals
- Maintenance of plant equipment or machineries on day to day basis
- Maintenance of plant equipment or machineries for long term basis
- Predicting and scheduling maintenance activities.
- Procurement of spare parts for maintenance activities and product packaging.
- Payment release of Procure material
- Storing and preservation of various procured raw material, spare parts and packaging material.
- Performance management of process operation
- Quality control of raw material, intermediates and product using laboratories or on line measurement
- Laboratories analysis for supporting production operation
- Research and Development of innovation and new products.
- Safety of operation and maintenance activities
- Compliance of environment and effluent discharge management
- Product packaging.
- Transportation or logistics of raw material and products.
- Marketing of product and intermediates products.
- HR Activities
- Finance Department having various activities

Chapter 3 – Data in the Chemical Industry

Artificial intelligence runs on data. In the chemical industry, data is everywhere—generated in laboratories, production plants, supply chains, and customer interactions. However, having vast amounts of data is not enough; the challenge lies in organizing, cleaning, and using it effectively.

3.1 Types of Data in the Chemical Industry

Chemical companies produce a rich variety of data types, each with its own format, frequency, and purpose.

Process Data

Process data are captured through thousands of sensors available in the plant in real time, these data are displayed through Distributed Control Systems (DCS), and Supervisory Control and Data Acquisition (SCADA) systems.

Examples: reactor temperature at different locations, pressure, flow rates, pH, energy consumption.

AI use case: Detecting process anomalies, predicting yield, optimizing control parameters.

Laboratory Data

Generated in R&D labs, Process analysis of different streams in plant and quality control labs.

Examples: spectroscopy readings, chromatographic profiles, Mass spectro meter for process constituents, PH particle size distribution, experimental yields.

AI use case: Accelerating formulation design, identifying patterns in experimental results.

Maintenance Data

Logs from equipment inspections, maintenance schedules, Online and offline vibration sensors and thermography.

AI use case: Predictive maintenance and failure mode analysis.

Supply Chain & Commercial Data

ERP system outputs, raw material pricing, sales orders, inventory levels, shipping routes.

Spare Part Prices, sales order, inventory level, delivery time of spares.

AI use case: Demand forecasting, procurement optimization, dynamic pricing.

External Data Sources

Weather data, commodity market trends, customer feedback, regulatory updates.

AI use case: Adjusting production based on forecasted demand or environmental conditions.

3.2 Data Challenges in the Chemical Industry

While chemical companies are data-rich, they often face barriers in its utilization, that limit AI's effectiveness:

Data Silos: Process control data may be stored separately from lab or supply chain data, making holistic analysis difficult. There are different systems of data like, process data are available in Distributed Control Systems or Data Acquisition Systems. These data are available in real time but they can not to be communicate with other data systems like Plant Log sheet, Shift log book or other Maintenance records or Lab Reporting Systems which is collected at much slower frequency than process data systems.

Inconsistent Formats: Different plants or departments may use incompatible systems or units of measure. Like Process data is available in digital form but are not able to communicate with due proprietary communication protocols. While Lab data is available in hard copy or MS office like Excel spreadsheet or Word documents. Similarly Maintenance records are available either in SAP system or physical hard Copy or MS office documents form.

Data Quality Issues: Sensor error exist even in best maintained plant due inherent nature of measurement, drift, missing values, human entry errors, and outdated records can make it very difficult or nearly impossible to use them for further processing for analysis. Even some Sensor location itself make data error prone and they do not have representative value of the process.

Limited Historical Records: Older plants may not have digital archives for past performance data.

Security and Privacy Concerns: Intellectual property and regulatory data require strict access controls.

3.3 Building the Data Foundation for AI

For AI to deliver value, data must be reliable, accessible, and well-structured. Key steps include:

Data Integration

Connecting different systems (DCS, LIMS, ERP) into unified platforms.

Using Industrial Internet of Things (IIoT) gateways to stream real-time data.

Data Cleaning and Validation

Removing outliers, filling missing values, calibrating sensors.

Implementing automated quality checks.

Data Storage and Management

Using secure cloud platforms or on-premise data lakes.

Implementing role-based access for sensitive information.

Recording units of measure, sampling frequency, and equipment IDs.

Ensuring datasets have proper labels for supervised machine learning.

Governance and Compliance

Defining data ownership and stewardship roles.

Ensuring compliance with regulations like REACH, OSHA, and environmental standards.

3.4 The Role of Domain Expertise

AI models can process vast datasets, but their effectiveness depends on context. In the chemical industry, process engineers, chemists, and plant operators provide critical insights into:

- Which variables truly influence yield or quality.
- How to interpret anomalies in the data.
- Which correlations are meaningful versus coincidental.

The most successful AI initiatives combine data science expertise with deep chemical process knowledge.

Chapter 4 – Machine Learning Applications in the Chemical Industry

Machine learning (ML) is the backbone of modern AI. While automation and process control have been part of chemical plants for decades, Machine Learning has improved process optimization. Earlier plant process data were being used for making process simulation model and then this model was being used for process optimization. With Introduction of AI model is being prepared without programming. Plant decision-making to a new level-learning from historical data and adapting to new conditions without explicit reprogramming. Without AI, making Process simulation model was difficult and costly, hence they were made only in the beginning of project and kept same even in changed conditions leading to ingress of error in computations.

4.1 What Machine Learning Brings to the Table

At its core, machine learning identifies patterns and relationships in data, enabling predictive and prescriptive insights.

In the chemical industry, this translates to:

Predicting outcomes before they happen (Production, Energy Consumption, yield, quality, equipment failure).

Optimizing processes dynamically as conditions change.

Discovering new chemical formulations faster than traditional experimentation.

4.2 Key Machine Learning Techniques for Chemical Applications

Supervised Learning

Description: Models learn from labeled data (input–output pairs).

Examples: Predicting product quality from process variables, forecasting energy consumption or forecasting production of products.

Common algorithms: Linear regression, decision trees, random forests, gradient boosting, neural networks.

Unsupervised Learning

Description: Models detect patterns in unlabeled data.

Examples: Clustering similar production batches, identifying unusual process behavior.

Common algorithms: K-means clustering, hierarchical clustering, principal component analysis (PCA).

Reinforcement Learning

Description: Models learn optimal actions through trial and error, guided by rewards.

Examples: Dynamic process control where the system adjusts parameters in real-time to maximize efficiency.

4.3 High-Impact Use Cases

Yield Prediction and Optimization

Challenge: Chemical yields vary due to feedstock quality, environmental conditions, and process fluctuations.

ML Solution: Predict yields based on historical process parameters and recommend adjustments.

Impact: Higher throughput, reduced waste.

Process Anomaly Detection

Challenge: Small deviations can cause large losses or safety hazards.

ML Solution: Real-time models flag abnormal patterns before alarms trigger.

Impact: Early intervention, improved safety.

Predictive Maintenance

Challenge: Unplanned equipment failures cause costly downtime.

ML Solution: Machine Vibration, Bearing temperature, and Discharge pressure sensor data feed into models that predict failure probabilities.

Impact: Maintenance scheduled before breakdowns, reduced spare part costs and avoid costly machine downtime.

Energy Optimization

Challenge: Energy is one of the largest operating costs in chemical plants.

ML Solution: Models identify optimal operating ranges for minimum energy use without compromising quality.

Impact: Lower utility costs, Reduced production cost, reduced CO_2 footprint.

Quality Classification

Challenge: Products must meet stringent quality specs.

ML Solution: Classification models sort batches into quality categories and identify root causes of defects.

Impact: Reduced rework, improved customer satisfaction.

R&D Acceleration

Challenge: New product development cycles are long and expensive.

ML Solution: Predictive models guide experiment design, narrowing down the most promising formulations.

Impact: Faster time-to-market, lower R&D costs.

4.4 Barriers to Adoption

While the potential is high, real-world adoption of ML in chemical plants faces:

Data limitations: Insufficient historical data or low-quality measurements.

Change management issues: Resistance from operators and engineers who trust established methods.

Model explainability: Regulatory and safety-critical contexts require interpretable models.

Integration complexity: Connecting ML models to existing process control systems can be challenging.

4.5 The Human–AI Partnership

Machine learning is not a replacement for human expertise—it is an amplifier. Successful applications pair:

AI's pattern recognition with

Human understanding of chemistry and engineering principles

Process engineers remain essential to validate model outputs, ensure safety, and guide strategic decisions.

Chapter 5 – Computer Vision in Chemical Operations

In the chemical industry, a significant portion of quality control, safety inspection, and maintenance activities relies on human visual inspection. With advances in computer vision (CV), Artificial Intelligence can now analyze images and videos with speed, precision, and consistency, reducing human error and enabling real-time monitoring.

5.1 What Is Computer Vision?

Computer vision is the field of AI that enables machines to interpret and analyze visual data—images, videos, or live camera feeds. Using deep learning algorithms, CV systems can detect objects, classify defects, monitor environments, and even measure physical attributes without manual intervention.

5.2 Sources of Visual Data in the Chemical Industry

Fixed Plant Cameras

Installed in production lines, reactors, storage areas, and loading bays.

Monitor operational status, detect leaks, continuity of operation, spillage of product from Belt conveyors or verify safety compliance.

Laboratory Imaging Systems

High-resolution microscopes, spectroscopy imaging, particle analyzers.

Generate data for quality control and formulation studies.

Example: Examination Gypsum crystal growth after crystallizers on Filter in Phosphoric acid plant

Mobile & Drone Cameras

Used for inspecting tall structures, pipelines, and remote facilities.

Capture images in hazardous or inaccessible areas.

Thermal and Infrared Imaging

Detect heat patterns in equipment, indicating possible faults or inefficiencies.

Example: Detection of tray conditions in distillation column or any tall column, Detection of condition of Baffles inside Heat Exchanger.

5.3 Key Applications of Computer Vision

Quality Control and Defect Detection

Example: Identifying surface imperfections in coated products, bubbles in polymers, or discoloration in batches.

AI Advantage: Continuous inspection at production speeds, detecting defects invisible to the human eye.

Safety Compliance Monitoring

Example: Detecting whether workers are wearing personal protective equipment (PPE) such as helmets, gloves, or safety goggles.

AI Advantage: Automated compliance checks without manual oversight.

Leak and Spill Detection

Example: Cameras linked to CV algorithms can spot oil spills, chemical leaks, or abnormal vapors.

AI Advantage: Real-time alerts prevent escalation into safety incidents.

Corrosion and Equipment Wear Analysis

Example: Drone images analyzed to detect corrosion on storage tanks, pipelines, or structural supports.

AI Advantage: Early intervention before structural failure.

Process Monitoring

Example: Tracking foam levels in reactors, crystal formation stages, or fluid color changes.

AI Advantage: Enables process optimization and consistency.

5.4 Technologies Behind Computer Vision

Convolutional Neural Networks (CNNs): The core architecture for image classification and object detection.

Object Detection Models: Algorithms like YOLO (You Only Look Once) or Faster R-CNN for identifying multiple objects in an image.

Image Segmentation: Techniques to locate and label each pixel of an object (useful for spill mapping or defect sizing).

Edge AI: Running CV models directly on cameras or local devices for real-time decision-making without cloud delays.

5.5 Benefits

Improved Product Quality: Fewer defects, better customer satisfaction.

Reduced Inspection Costs: Less reliance on manual inspectors.

Enhanced Safety: Proactive hazard detection.

Downtime Reduction: Early equipment fault detection prevents costly stoppages.

Progress reporting of Project construction without or less reliance on manual inspectors.

5.6 Implementation Considerations

Data Requirements: High-quality labeled images are needed to train models effectively.

Environmental Conditions: Lighting, dust, and camera positioning affect accuracy.

Integration: CV systems must link with Manufacturing Execution Systems (MES) or Distributed Control Systems (DCS).

Change Management: Operators need training to trust and act on CV-generated alerts.

Chapter 6 – Natural Language Processing in the Chemical Industry

While much of the chemical industry's data is numerical or visual, an enormous amount exists in text form—technical reports, patents, safety datasheets, regulatory filings, market intelligence, research papers, and even operator logs. Natural Language Processing (NLP) is the branch of AI that enables machines to understand, analyze, and generate human language, making it possible to extract insights from these unstructured text sources.

6.1 What Is Natural Language Processing?

NLP combines linguistics, computer science, and machine learning to:

Parse and interpret human language

Extract meaning, entities, and relationships

Generate text summaries or responses

Translate between languages or jargon types

In chemical operations, NLP bridges the gap between human-written knowledge and machine-driven decision-making.

6.2 Key Text Data Sources in the Chemical Industry

Research Literature

Scientific papers, conference proceedings, and journals contain valuable insights on new reactions, catalysts, and materials.

NLP Use Case: Automatically extract reaction conditions, yields, or material properties.

Patents

Patent databases contain detailed process descriptions and novel chemical formulations.

NLP Use Case: Identify competitive threats, detect expired patents for potential adoption.

Regulatory Documents

REACH, OSHA, EPA filings, and environmental compliance reports are often long and complex.

NLP Use Case: Extract relevant compliance clauses and safety thresholds.

Material Safety Data Sheets (MSDS)

Safety, handling, and disposal information.

NLP Use Case: Create searchable safety databases and real-time hazard alerts.

Plant Logs and Maintenance Notes

Operators' shift reports and maintenance logs often contain informal but critical observations.

NLP Use Case: Identify recurring equipment issues or process anomalies.

Market and Supplier Reports

Contain pricing trends, demand forecasts, and geopolitical risks.

NLP Use Case: Automated extraction of price trends and supply chain risks.

6.3 Core NLP Applications in the Chemical Industry

Information Extraction (IE)

Automatically pulling structured data from text.

Example: Extracting "temperature = 85°C" and "pressure = 2.5 bar" from experimental write-ups.

Text Summarization

Condensing lengthy reports into actionable briefs.

Example: Summarizing 50-page regulatory filings into a 1-page compliance checklist.

Semantic Search

Finding documents based on meaning, not just keywords.

Example: Searching for "high-yield catalysts for propylene polymerization" and retrieving relevant R&D documents even if they use different wording.

Sentiment and Opinion Analysis

Gauging supplier feedback, employee safety concerns, or customer satisfaction from text data.

Machine Translation for Technical Text

Translating chemical documentation between languages while preserving scientific accuracy.

Question-Answering Systems

Enabling engineers to query internal knowledge bases in plain language ("What solvents are compatible with polymer X?").

6.4 Benefits of NLP in Chemical Operations

Faster Knowledge Discovery: Reduces time spent manually searching through documents.

Enhanced Compliance: Automatically monitors for regulatory changes.

Improved Collaboration: Breaks down language and terminology barriers.

Competitive Intelligence: Tracks competitors' patent and research activities.

6.5 Challenges to Adoption

Technical Jargon and Ambiguity: NLP must be trained on domain-specific chemical terminology.

Data Privacy: Proprietary research and customer contracts require secure handling.

Document Quality: Scanned or handwritten reports may need preprocessing via Optical Character Recognition (OCR).

Interpretation Accuracy: Misinterpreted text could lead to regulatory or operational errors.

6.6 Future Directions for NLP in Chemicals

Generative AI for Experiment Design: Suggesting new reaction pathways from literature.

Automated Regulatory Auditing: AI agents that proactively flag compliance risks.

Voice-to-Text Process Monitoring: Capturing verbal operator notes for real-time analysis.

Integration with Digital Twins: Feeding extracted text parameters into process simulations.

Part Two
AI in Core Plant Operations

Chapter 7 – R&D and Product Development with AI

Research and Development (R&D) is the lifeline of the chemical industry. It drives the creation of new molecules, catalysts, formulations, and processes that underpin innovation across multiple sectors—pharmaceuticals, agrochemicals, plastics, coatings, specialty chemicals, and energy solutions. However, chemical R&D has traditionally been resource-intensive, time-consuming, and expensive. The complexity of chemical reactions, the unpredictability of molecular behavior, and the sheer scale of experimentation required often lead to long development cycles and high costs.

Artificial Intelligence (AI) has emerged as a transformative force in chemical R&D. By leveraging machine learning (ML), deep learning, natural language processing (NLP), robotics, and digital twins, chemical companies can drastically accelerate discovery, reduce costs, and improve sustainability. AI can surf through millions of possible molecular combinations, optimize reaction conditions, and even design entirely new materials that would have been unimaginable through traditional methods.

This chapter examines the evolution of R&D, the current status of AI adoption, key technologies, applications, benefits, challenges, and the future of AI in R&D for the chemical industry. It also integrates structured insights from both concise and detailed drafts to provide a comprehensive perspective. Flowcharts, comparison tables, and a roadmap infographic have been included to guide readers in understanding the transformative role of AI.

7.1 The Traditional R&D Cycle in Chemicals

The conventional R&D cycle involves several sequential stages

1. Literature & Patent Review

2. Hypothesis Formulation
3. Laboratory Experiment
4. Data analysis
5. Scale-up trials
6. Commercialization

While effective, this process is often linear and resource-intensive. Many experimental pathways are tested before the optimal one is found, leading to high time and cost investments.

TRADITIONAL AI-DRIVEN R&D CYCLE IN CHEMICAL INDUSTRY

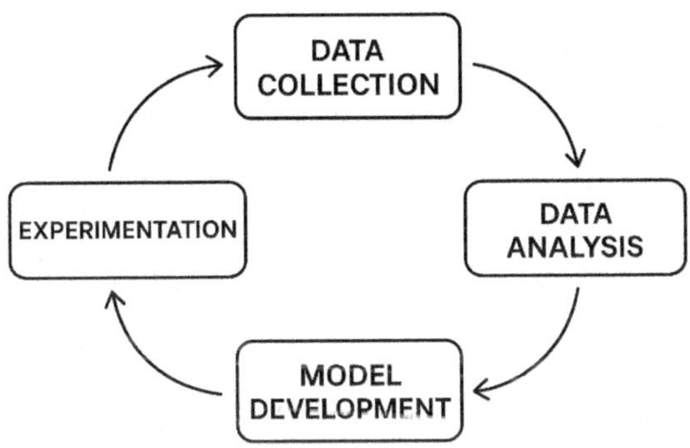

7.2 How AI Transforms R&D

AI shifts R&D from trial-and-error to data-driven hypothesis testing. By learning from existing datasets—internal experimental results, external literature, and simulation outputs—AI can:

• Predict promising formulations or compounds before physical testing.

• Model reaction outcomes under different conditions.

• Identify hidden correlations between molecular structures and material properties.

• Guide experiment design to focus on the highest-probability successes.

7.3 Key AI Technologies in Chemical R&D

1. Machine Learning for Property Prediction

- Predicts melting points, solubility, stability, or reaction yields from molecular descriptors.
- Example: Random forests or neural networks trained on historical compound data.

2. Generative AI for Molecule and Material Design

- Uses algorithms like Generative Adversarial Networks (GANs) or variational autoencoders (VAEs) to propose entirely new chemical structures.
- Example: Designing new catalysts or polymers with targeted properties.

3. Natural Language Processing for Knowledge Mining

- Automatically extracts relevant synthesis conditions or safety data from research papers and patents.
- Example: Quickly identifying all literature-reported catalysts for a given reaction.

4. AI-Driven Simulation and Modeling

- Combines quantum chemistry, molecular dynamics, and process simulation with AI models for faster computation.
- Example: Predicting material performance under extreme temperatures without expensive lab tests.

7.4 Practical R&D Use Cases

1. New Polymer Development – AI models predict tensile strength, thermal resistance, and chemical compatibility before synthesis.

2. Catalyst Discovery – AI analyzes thousands of potential catalyst structures to shortlist those with optimal activity and selectivity.

3. Formulation Optimization – AI evaluates ingredient ratios for paints, coatings, or adhesives to balance performance and cost.

4. Green Chemistry Initiatives – AI recommends alternative reagents or solvents to reduce environmental impact while maintaining yield.

5. Drug and Agrochemical Development – AI accelerates the identification of active ingredients with desired efficacy and safety profiles.

7.5 Benefits of AI in R&D

• Reduced Time-to-Market: Faster candidate identification and testing.

• Lower Costs: Fewer failed experiments and wasted materials.

• Higher Innovation Rate: Exploration of chemical spaces too vast for human-led testing.

• Improved Sustainability: Design of eco-friendly products from the start.

7.6 Challenges of AI in R&D

Adopting AI in R&D faces hurdles:

- Data Quality: Experimental data can be incomplete or inconsistent.
- Integration Issues: Linking AI platforms with existing lab systems.
- Skills Gap: Chemists may lack AI expertise; collaboration with data scientists is essential.
- High Costs: AI tools and infrastructure require significant investment.
- Interpretability: Lack of transparency in AI decision-making may limit trust.
- IP Concerns: Managing intellectual property when AI designs new molecules.

7.7 Roadmap for Implementing AI in R&D

Step 1: Digitize laboratory records and ensure data quality.

Step 2: Start with pilot AI projects in molecule design or catalyst development.

Step 3: Build interdisciplinary teams (chemists, data scientists, engineers).

Step 4: Scale successful pilots across the R&D value chain.

Step 5: Train staff and embed a culture of data-driven research.

Step 6: Continuously update and refine AI models with new data.

7.8 Case Studies

Case Study 1: CHEMICAL GIANT A used AI to discover advanced materials with improved energy storage capabilities, cutting discovery time in half.

Case Study 2: Chemical Giant B employed AI-driven catalyst modeling, resulting in significant cost savings and efficiency improvements in polyethylene production.

Case Study 3: Chemical Giant C applied AI-based NLP for literature mining, accelerating pharmaceutical-related chemical discoveries.

7.9 The Future of AI in Chemical R&D

The future developments include:

- Self-Driving Laboratories: Fully autonomous labs conducting research 24/7.
- Quantum Computing + AI: Revolutionizing molecular simulations beyond classical limits.
- Collaborative AI Platforms: Enabling cross-border R&D collaboration.

- Sustainable Innovation: AI supporting eco-friendly solutions such as CO2 utilization, bio-based feedstocks, and circular economy chemicals.
- Personalized Chemistry: Designing chemicals for highly specific applications in real time.

Chapter 8 - AI in Process Optimization for the Chemical Industry

8.1 Introduction

Process optimization has always been central to the chemical industry, where margins are tight, energy usage is high, and safety is paramount. Traditional approaches—such as statistical process control, Six Sigma, and advanced process control—have yielded significant gains, but in the era of digital transformation, artificial intelligence (AI) is emerging as a game-changer. AI is enabling chemical companies to maximize yield, improve energy efficiency, reduce emissions, and enhance safety at unprecedented level.

8.2 Present Status of Process Optimization in the Chemical Industry

The chemical industry operates some of the most complex continuous and batch processes in the world. From refineries and petrochemical plants to fertilizers, specialty chemicals, and polymers, optimization has been driven largely by human expertise supported by digital control systems. Distributed Control Systems (DCS) and Supervisory Control and Data Acquisition (SCADA) platforms are well established. Model Predictive Control (MPC) has been widely used for decades. Yet, these methods depend heavily on a human excellence. Where process plant model is identified based on step test or any other disturbance test. These models can be statistical or from first principal model or combination of both. Once these models is identified, these model are used for advance control to control the plant to minimize the variation in process. The similar or different model is used to optimize the plant variable to achieve maximum production, or minimum specific energy consumption to gain maximum financial benefit, hence they generate set point to controllers for maintaining individual variable. Main limitation was model identification was very costly and most of the time it was done only once at start of the project implementation. Hence prediction errors used to creep in after some period of time

8.3 AI Applications in Process Optimization

AI allows optimization to go beyond the limits of traditional models. Some of the most impactful applications include:

1. Advanced Process Control (APC) Reinvented

- AI-enhanced controllers can adapt dynamically to changing process conditions, handling nonlinearities better than traditional MPC.
- Reinforcement learning agents are being tested to optimize reaction temperatures, pressure levels, and catalyst lifetimes.

2. Real-Time Monitoring and Predictive Analytics

- Machine learning models can analyze thousands of sensor readings simultaneously, identifying patterns invisible to human operators.
- Predictive models can anticipate process upsets, equipment fouling, or catalyst deactivation, enabling proactive intervention.

3. Energy Optimization

- AI can continuously analyze energy consumption across distillation columns, heat exchangers, compressors, and boilers.
- Plants can reduce energy intensity by 5–15% by using AI-driven recommendations to adjust process parameters in real time.

4. Yield and Throughput Enhancement

- In batch processes, AI can optimize recipe parameters, agitation rates, and reaction times for maximum yield.

- For continuous operations, AI models can fine-tune operating windows that maximize throughput without compromising product quality.

5. Safety and Environmental Compliance

- AI-powered systems can simulate thousands of "what-if" scenarios to predict runaway reactions, leaks, or emissions exceedances.
- Regulatory compliance is strengthened through real-time AI-driven monitoring of effluents, emissions, and flare systems.

6. Digital Twins in Process Industries

- A digital twin is a virtual replica of the plant, combining physics-based models with AI-based learning models.
- These twins allow scenario testing, predictive maintenance, and process reconfiguration without risking real-world downtime.

8.4 Case Examples

- Chemical Giant A: Using AI-driven process optimization in steam crackers has saved millions in energy costs annually.
- Chemical Giant B: Digital twins combined with machine learning are used to optimize polymerization reactions, reducing variability in product grades.
- Chemical Giant C: Pilot programs applying AI for refinery optimization have improved crude blending efficiency and distillation performance.

8.5 Challenges in Deploying AI for Process Optimization

1. Data Availability and Quality

- Sensor calibration errors, missing values, and inconsistent data formats often limit the effectiveness of AI models.

Sensor data, even if calibrated frequently contain errors and most of the times does not obey first principle of Mass Balance, Energy

Balance or Momentum Balance, and most of the time require data smoothening or reconciliation software before using them for further application. Particularly for process optimization model, while advance control model can tolerate model error to some extent.

2. Integration with Legacy Systems

- Many plants run on decades-old DCS/PLC systems that are not natively designed for AI integration.

3. Trust and Interpretability

- Operators are hesitant to adopt AI recommendations without clear explanations of the reasoning behind them.

4. Cybersecurity and Safety Concerns

- Connecting AI to real-time process controls increases vulnerability to cyberattacks.

5. Workforce Readiness

- Upskilling chemical engineers and operators to collaborate with AI systems is a major organizational challenge.

8.6 Future Outlook

AI in process optimization will increasingly be integrated with other technologies:

- Autonomous Operations: AI will move from recommendation systems to autonomous process adjustments under human oversight.
- Green Optimization: Carbon reduction and circular economy goals will drive AI applications toward minimizing waste and energy use.
- Edge AI: Running AI models directly on industrial edge devices will enable faster decision-making with lower latency.
- Hybrid Models: Combining first-principles chemical engineering models with AI/ML models will deliver the best of both worlds.

Chapter 9 - AI in Maintenance Department

Overview

Maintenance is the quiet backbone of the chemical industry. When assets run reliably, plants meet production targets, uphold process safety, reduce environmental incidents, and protect margins. When maintenance is reactive or poorly coordinated, the consequences are immediate: unplanned downtime, quality losses, safety risks, and energy waste. Artificial Intelligence (AI) is reshaping maintenance from a calendar-driven cost center into a data-driven, risk-aware value creator. This chapter explains the present state of AI in maintenance, its challenges in the chemical context, and a practical future roadmap—so a reader can move from pilot to scaled, sustainable impact.

9.1Why AI in Maintenance Matters for Chemical Plants

- Safety and compliance: Many assets are part of safety instrumented functions or affect critical barriers. AI can support early anomaly detection and help maintenance teams prioritize safety-critical work orders.
- Economics: Across rotating equipment (pumps, compressors, blowers), static equipment (vessels, exchangers, pipelines), and utilities (boilers, chillers, cooling towers), predictive maintenance (PdM) reduces unplanned downtime, optimizes spares, and improves overall equipment effectiveness (OEE).
- Energy and emissions: Poorly performing equipment consumes more energy and may drive emissions or flaring. AI-guided maintenance reduces leakages, energy, fouling, and off-spec operations.
- Workforce leverage: Skilled maintenance resources are constrained of skill of manpower deployed. AI copilots,

standardized diagnostics, and autonomous inspections multiply human capability without compromising judgment.

9.2Present Status—What's Working Today

9.2.1 Data foundations in brownfield plants

- OSIsoft PI and other data historians hold decades of sensor data; CMMS/EAM (e.g., SAP PM, Maximo) hold work history; DCS/SCADA capture real-time operations; handheld routes hold vibration/ultrasound; and Lab Information Management System holds quality and process chemistry data. AI value today comes from integrating these islands.
- Edge computing is common for high-frequency vibration, acoustic, and video streams where bandwidth or latency is a constraint. Cloud analytics handle heavy training and fleet benchmarking.

9.2.2 Common AI use cases in maintenance

- Rotating equipment health: Anomaly detection on pumps and compressors using multivariate time-series from pressure, flow, temperature, vibration, and motor currents. Models detect incipient cavitation, misalignment, bearing wear, and seal degradation.
- Heat exchanger fouling prediction: Time-series + physics constraints estimate fouling resistance and forecast cleaning windows to minimize energy penalties and production shutdowns.
- Steam trap and compressed-air leak detection: Acoustic classification models and continuous ultrasonic sensors identify failed-open/failed-closed traps and leaks at scale.
- Corrosion and thickness monitoring: Models combine ultrasonic thickness readings, corrosion coupons, process

conditions, and materials data to forecast corrosion rates and plan inspections.

- Valve stiction and control loop health: AI flags sticky valves, oscillatory loops, and poorly tuned controllers impacting product variability and asset stress.
- Computer vision for inspections: Cameras and drones detect leaks, frost buildup on cryogenic lines, insulation damage, corrosion under insulation (CUI) signatures, and gauge readings.
- NLP on maintenance logs: Language models extract failure modes, parts, and causes from free-text work orders to enrich FMEA libraries and improve spares planning.
- Parts/supply optimization: Forecasting models predict spare consumption, lead-time risks, and stockout probability to right-size inventory and reduce expediting.
- Technician guidance: Copilots suggest likely root causes and next-best actions based on history, manuals, P&IDs, and similar incidents across the fleet.

9.3 Core Data and Modeling for Chemical Maintenance

9.3.1 Data map for a typical site

- Time series: flows, pressures, temperatures, vibration (acceleration/velocity/enveloping), motor current signature analysis (MCSA), ultrasonic sensors, acoustic microphones, thermal imaging derived metrics.
- Events: alarms, trips, interlocks, overrides, maintenance work orders, operator rounds, near-miss reports.
- Static/reference: equipment master data (tag/asset hierarchy), nameplate, P&IDs, materials, design conditions.
- Context: product slates, campaigns, feedstock quality, ambient conditions, shift schedules.

- Quality and lab: viscosity, composition, Ph, acidity, solids, corrosion potential.
- Energy: steam balances, electrical KPIs, cooling water metrics, furnace/boiler efficiency.

9.3.2 Modeling tactics for low-label environments

- Start unsupervised: multivariate autoencoders or isolation forests to find deviations.
- Add weak labels: use rule-based "silver labels" such as high vibration + rising bearing temperature to seed supervised learners.
- Semi-supervised and positive–unlabeled learning for rare failures.
- Use simulation and physics to generate synthetic failures (e.g., imposed leak, increased fouling resistance) for training and stress-testing.
- Human-in-the-loop for adjudication to prevent model drift and alert fatigue.

9.4Business Case and Value Proof

9.4.1 Typical value levers

- Reduced unplanned downtime on bad actors (compressors, critical pumps, extruders).
- Lower maintenance expenditure from condition-based intervals vs fixed-time overhauls.
- Energy savings from timely cleaning (exchangers), seal replacements, or leak repairs.
- Lower spares and working capital through risk-informed stocking.
- Extended asset life via early detection of destructive regimes (cavitation, dry gas seal failure).

9.4.2 KPIs to track

- Reliability: MTBF, MTTR, availability, bad-actor downtime.
- Planning & scheduling: schedule compliance, wrench time, backlog age.
- Alert performance: precision/recall, lead time to failure, engineer acceptance rate, rework rate.
- Financials: cost avoidance vs baseline, inventory turns, energy intensity improvement.
- Safety/environment: leak counts, flare events avoided, near-misses related to equipment failure.

9.4.3 ROI framing

- Identify top 10% critical assets that drive 60–70% of downtime cost.
- Quantify baseline: last 24–36 months of failures, durations, and costs.
- Attribute value to avoided events with conservative factors (e.g., 50% of predicted saves credited until maturity).
- Include enablement costs: sensors, connectivity, licenses, integration, and change management—not just model development.

9.5Implementation Roadmap for a Chemical Site

9.5.1 Identify What is Maturity model Level in Plant

- Level 0—Reactive: Break-fix, minimal condition monitoring.
- Level 1—Instrumented: Basic vibration routes, handheld thermography, CMMS discipline.
- Level 2—Connected: Historian + CMMS integration; automated data quality checks; first unsupervised anomaly detection.

- Level 3—Predictive and risk-based: Fleet models, hybrid physics–ML, RBM scheduling, closed-loop learning.
- Level 4—Autonomous assistance: Technician copilots, drone/robot inspections, continuous optimization loops with human approval.

Then try to improve upon

9.5.2 First 100 days of Implementation

- Baseline: Quantify downtime cost, identify bad actors, assemble cross-functional team (Reliability, Maintenance, Ops, Process, IT/OT, Safety).
- Data plumbing: Set up historian access, CMMS extract, asset hierarchy normalization, and data quality pipeline.
- Quick wins: Steam-trap survey with acoustic AI; pump anomaly detection on top 20 critical pumps; NLP to standardize failure codes from logs.
- Governance: Define alert review acceptance criteria, and how model-generated insights turn into work orders.
- Training: Upskill planners and technicians; pair reliability engineers with data scientists.

9.5.3 Scale-out

- Pattern libraries: "Model recipes" for common equipment classes—pumps, exchangers, compressors, cooling towers—accelerate replication.
- Asset templates: Predefined tags, features, and alert rules so every new pump doesn't start from zero.
- Center of Excellence (CoE): Curate best practices, tools, and vendor frameworks; run champion–challenger evaluations; manage model registry.
- Contracting model: Blend vendor solutions (sensors + analytics) with in-house models for strategic assets; ensure IP and data rights are clear.

- Change management: Recognize and reward usage—track how often AI alerts prevent failures and highlight technician contributions.

9.6Chemical-Industry Case examples

9.6.1 Pump seal failure on aromatic unit

- Context: Multiple mechanical seal failures causing environmental incidents and expensive cleanups.
- Approach: Fused vibration, seal flush temperature, and differential pressure across pump; unsupervised detector raised residuals above threshold 12–36 hours before failure.
- Outcome: Planned changeouts reduced seal failures by ~60%; added nitrogen purge interlocks based on insights.

9.6.2 Heat exchanger fouling in ethylene oxide unit

- Context: Rising energy intensity and throughput loss due to fouled exchangers.
- Approach: Physics–ML hybrid estimated fouling resistance and projected optimal cleaning window given energy prices and production plan.
- Outcome: 8–12% energy savings and improved campaign length; optimized cleaning during low-demand windows.

9.6.3 Steam trap failure detection in a utilities network

- Context: High steam losses and water hammer risks.
- Approach: Acoustic classification using edge devices; weekly automated report with trap ID, likelihood of failure, and priority.
- Outcome: Payback in months; fewer pressure excursions and better condensate return quality.

9.6.4 Corrosion under insulation (CUI) risk ranking

- Context: Unplanned leaks and integrity risks in insulated piping.

- Approach: Computer vision on drone imagery + weather and process data to rank likely CUI hotspots; inspections focused accordingly.
- Outcome: Reduced inspection scope by 30% with higher hit rate on genuine defects.

9.6.5 NLP on maintenance history to improve spares

- Context: Frequent stockouts and overstocking of critical parts.
- Approach: Language model normalized free-text into ISO 14224-like codes; demand forecasting adjusted min/max levels by risk.
- Outcome: Better service levels and 15–25% reduction in tied-up capital for certain categories.

9.7 Challenges Specific to Chemical Maintenance

9.7.1 Data challenges

- Sensor drift and calibration gaps; mixed sampling rates; missing data during turnarounds; historian tag changes without notice.
- Rare events: high-consequence failures are (fortunately) uncommon—labels are scarce and often inconsistent.
- Context blindness: Models trained on steady-state struggle during startups, grade changes, or abnormal operations.
- Multi-causality: The same symptom (e.g., high vibration) can have many different causes; naive classifiers overfit.

9.7.2 Organizational and process challenges

- Siloed ownership: Reliability vs Maintenance vs Operations vs Process Engineering leading to unclear accountability for AI alerts.
- Alert fatigue: Too many weak alerts quickly erode trust. Without root-cause narratives and recommended actions, adoption stalls.

- Skills gap: Data fluency varies; lack of translators who speak both engineering and data science.
- Change control: Introducing model-driven recommendations without MOC can run afoul of safety culture.
- Vendor sprawl: Point solutions proliferate without integration into CMMS and historian, creating shadow systems and duplicated alerts.

9.7.3 Technology and governance challenges

- Integration into outside networks and cybersecurity boundaries can be slow.
- Model explainability: Black-box models are hard to defend in HAZOPs, audits, and incident investigations.
- Reliability of AI itself: Sensor faults or data pipeline outages can silence alerts ("failure to alert" risk).
- Regulatory and standards alignment: Aligning with ISO 55000 (asset management), ISO 14224 (reliability data), ISA-95/ISA-88 (integration), and IEC 62443 (security) requires discipline.
- Ethics and workforce impact: Ensure AI augments technicians; avoid surveillance misuse; maintain fair task assignment.

9.8Practical Controls to Mitigate Challenges

- Start with bad-actor assets and define crisp "stop-loss" rules: who sees alerts, escalation paths, and when to switch to safe-state operation.
- Use hybrid models with physics constraints; include uncertainty bounds and confidence intervals in dashboards.
- Implement alert quality gates: Minimum precision, minimum lead time, and peer review by reliability engineers before sending it to production deployment.

- Create an "AI bill of materials": data lineage, model version, training dates, features, assumptions, and known limitations per model.
- Run periodic model PHA (Process Hazard Analysis) for safety-critical recommendations; include "what if model silent/incorrect?" scenarios.
- Build a labeled-outcome loop: Every alert outcome logged in CMMS with reason codes (true positive/false positive/near miss/unknown).
- Invest in a single pane of glass: Reliability dashboard that blends AI alerts, work orders, and asset KPIs; avoid multiple alert inboxes.
- Build skills: Pair apprenticeships—data scientist shadows reliability engineer and vice versa for one quarter.

9.9 Architecture Blueprint

- Edge layer: Condition monitoring devices for vibration/acoustics/thermal; PLC/DCS taps; on-edge filtering and feature extraction for high-rate streams.
- Data platform: Historian replication, time-series store, data lake house; metadata catalog with asset hierarchy (equipment–tag mapping).
- Model services: Feature store, model registry, automated retraining, drift detection, champion–challenger release pipeline.
- Integration: CMMS/EAM connectors (notifications, work orders, parts); messaging bus for alerts; role-based access control and audit trails.
- Visualization: Reliability cockpit with risk-ranked asset list, explainable narratives, and recommended actions; mobile views for technicians.

9.10 Build vs Buy—How to Choose

- Buy when speed matters for standard problems (steam traps, bearing faults, leak detection); vendors ship sensors + analytics + support.
- Build when your process physics or failure modes are unique and confer advantage; keep IP in-house for crown-jewel assets.
- Hybrid is common: standard vendor packages plus a site/Fleet model layer for cross-asset learning and unified governance.
- Evaluate vendors on: integration ease with your historian/CMMS, alert precision/recall benchmarks, explainability tools, mobile workflows, cybersecurity posture, and commercial flexibility.

9.11 The Future of AI in Chemical Maintenance

9.11.1 Foundation models for time series and maintenance text

- Pretrained models on multi-plant, multi-asset datasets will provide out-of-the-box anomaly detection and failure narratives, fine-tuned with your site data.
- Language–time-series fusion: Models that read tags, alarms, and work orders together to propose root causes and safe actions with uncertainty.
- Multimodal digital assistants: Live P&ID understanding, photo/video analysis, and procedure step-checking through AR headsets.

9.11.2 Autonomous inspection ecosystems

- Drones and ground robots perform repetitive rounds, thermography, acoustic scans, and leak detection in hazardous areas.

- AI prioritizes inspection routes by dynamic risk; findings auto-generate work notifications with rich context (images, audio, measurements).

9.11.3 Physics-informed twins and prescriptive maintenance

- High-fidelity digital twins simulate degradation and recommend maintenance windows that co-optimize safety, energy, throughput, and emissions.
- Prescriptive actions (e.g., reduce recycle ratio, change seal flush) issued with guardrails and human approval, closing the loop from prediction to action.

9.11.4 Trust, safety, and regulation by design

- Model cards and safety cases will be standard, especially for assets affecting safety barriers or environmental discharge.
- Third-party validation and periodic recertification for models used in safety-critical decisions.
- Privacy-preserving learning (federated, differential privacy) across company fleets to share learnings without sharing raw data.

9.11.5 Talent and ways of working

- Maintenance engineers become "AI-enabled reliability leaders," fluent in data storytelling and ethics.
- New roles: model reliability engineer, data product owner, and inspection automation lead.
- Upskilling pathways via micro-credentials and vendor academies integrated into competency matrices.

9.12 Getting Started—A Checklist for Plant Leaders

- Define the "North Star": reduce unplanned downtime by X%, cut energy intensity by Y%, improve schedule compliance by Z%.

- Pick 2–3 use cases with line-of-sight value and strong data: e.g., pump health, steam traps.
- Stand up the data backbone: historian-to-lake, CMMS integration, asset hierarchy, and data quality monitors.
- Establish governance: alert review board, MOC for models, cybersecurity gates.
- Prove value in 90 days with transparent metrics and technician-in-the-loop.
- Scale with templates, CoE, and contract frameworks.

9.13 Practical guide for AI Automation of Maintenance Department

A. Day to day maintenance

Current status

Daily Jobs

- Currently a daily job list is being prepared by operation department and handed over to maintenance for job to be under taken today, based on availability of manpower and effect on plant operation, if machine is handed over to maintenance for a period of X hours.
- Backlog list of job of maintenance is also prepared.
- Maintenance department takes up the job and complete the possible job on the same day and handover the equipment to user department for inspection/checking of performance and production department start using. The remaining job either carried over to next day or scheduled for convenient time.
- A shutdown job list is prepared by user department and maintenance department for any available breakdown when jobs are undertaken with time limitation, manpower and contract manpower and spare part availability.
- Maintenance Engineer also plans for availability of spare parts.

- Maintenance engineer also line up contract for under taking job with contract manpower.

Short shutdown Maintenance

In case of any breakdown in any machinery or any break down in upstream plant or downstream plant. There is a opportunity to undertake the job which cannot be done during normal plant operation.

Hence on availability such short shut down an immediate job list is prepared and maintenance undertake few jobs, which can be completed within available period, subject to availability of spare parts.

Annual Shutdown Maintenance

User Department and Maintenance department prepare a Annual shutdown job list.

Maintenance Department also plan the spare part availability.

Generate requirements for spare part and equipment to be replaced in annual shutdown and raise requirement to procurement group.

Maintenance engineer also lineup contract for job planned to be under taken during Annual shutdown with contract manpower.

Maintenance department prepare yearly budget for Daily job, short shutdown job and annual maintenance Jobs.

Possible effect of Artificial Intelligence

AI can keep records of daily job list after taking input from production and other department and sent to relevant maintenance (Mechanical, Electrical, Instrument and Civil) personnel and maintenance head as well as the plant in charge, this includes back log of jobs

AI can prepare the job list to be undertaken today based present manpower and present contractor manpower and priority of jobs and availability of spare.

AI can plan for availability of spare part based on predicted consumption.

AI can predict spare's quantity and generate requirement for not available spare parts to procurement team.

AI can also assist Maintenance Engineers to line up necessary contract for jobs to be undertaking on day to day basis, for short shutdown and during Annual shutdown.

In the event of breakdown, AI can prepare break down job list instantaneously and based on estimated available time, manpower and spare part availability. AI can ensure the best usage of breakdown for carry out maintenance job in the plant.

During this breakdown possibility of availability of spare parts from other sources can also be checked.

Planning Annual shutdown

- AI can prepare job list for shutdown
- AI can generate Material requirement for the job.
- AI can help in procuring above material.
- AI can help in creating Job execution details.
- AI can help in generating services requirement for the jobs.
- AI can help in generating services order for the jobs.
- AI can help in consolidating general item procurement for entire complex.
- AI can help in procurement of above material
- AI can help in prepare consolidated list of general services requirement for entire chemical complex
- AI can help in placement of service order for general services requirement
- AI can help in issuing alerts for procurement action delay.
- AI can help in issuing alerts for delivery delay.
- AI can help in issuing alerts for inspection delays.
- AI can help in issuing alerts for delays in job execution

- AI can help in preparing contractor loading during annual shutdown, so that they do not book more jobs than their capacity during annual shutdown.
- AI can give suggestion of big jobs to be undertaken by outside contractor (Who come to site only for this job) to reduce load on local contractor and also for betterment of quality jobs.
- AI can help in scheduling general services, like scaffolding, insulation, compress air requirement, during long shutdown for better utilization of the same.

AI can have role in maintenance of plant equipment or machineries on day to day basis also.

Current status of rotating machinery maintenance.

- Jobs are carried out and history of breakdown is maintained in the history book of each machinery is maintained.
- Data of machine like bearing temperatures, vibration data are collected and if any abnormality in data is identified.
- Online data for machinery is transmitted to special group responsible for analyzing it.
- The report generated by them are reported back to plant maintenance group for job planning.
- Inspection report like thickness testing of pipe, bends and tubes are recorded for observation or action.
- history of running machine alignment is maintained.
- Component breakdown analysis is carried out to predict the next failure manually.
- Preventive maintenance jobs are planned based on abnormality and prediction.

AI can help in maintenance of Running machinery in following way.

- with better prediction of component failure with advanced analysis of failure

- Automated inspection for faster identification of abnormality.
- Automated camera or drone inspection.
- More accurate failure prediction
- Keeping tab on time available till next failure
- Maintenance engineer can better plan the job.

Appendix A: Glossary

- PdM (Predictive Maintenance): Maintenance based on predicted failure risk rather than fixed intervals.
- RBM (Risk-Based Maintenance): Prioritizing maintenance by consequence and likelihood of failure.
- MTBF/MTTR: Mean time between failures/mean time to repair.
- MCSA: Motor Current Signature Analysis for electric motor diagnostics.
- CUI: Corrosion Under Insulation.
- MOC: Management of Change.
- PSSR: Pre-Startup Safety Review.
- CoE: Center of Excellence.

Appendix B: Sample Alert Quality Criteria

- Minimum precision (e.g., ≥70%) over last 90 days.
- Minimum average lead time to failure (e.g., ≥12 hours) for targeted modes.
- Clear narrative with top contributing features and recommended actions.
- Outcome logging completeness ≥90% in CMMS.

Chapter 10 - AI in Quality Control for the Chemical Industry

10.1 Introduction

In the chemical industry, maintaining product quality is critical. From petrochemicals to specialty chemicals and consumer products, quality control (QC) ensures that the end products meet stringent regulatory standards, safety requirements, and customer expectations. Traditionally, QC involved manual sampling, inspections, and laboratory testing, often at various stages of production. However, with advancements in artificial intelligence (AI), the chemical industry is transitioning to more precise, automated, and data-driven methods of ensuring product quality.

AI technologies are revolutionizing quality control by providing real-time, data-driven insights, improving accuracy, and enabling predictive maintenance. AI can identify defects, optimize processes, and maintain consistency, minimizing variability. This chapter explores how AI is applied to quality control in the chemical industry, examining current practices, applications, and future potential.

10.2 Current Status of Quality Control Practices

The chemical industry is characterized by complex production processes, which often involve large-scale continuous and batch production. Traditionally, quality control has relied on manual testing and periodic sampling, which may introduce human error, delay feedback, and increase costs.

Key issues faced in traditional QC include:

Time delays between product sampling and lab results and consequent corrective action.

Variability in product quality due to inconsistent environmental and operational conditions.

Difficulty in real-time adjustments to the process based on quality findings.

High costs related to manual inspection and testing.

Historically, chemical plants used statistical process control (SPC) to monitor process stability and variability. While effective, SPC is reactive, offering limited insight into potential deviations before they occur. With the advancement of AI, the potential to move from reactive QC to predictive and real-time quality assurance has opened up new possibilities for improved efficiency and product consistency.

10.3 AI Applications in Quality Control

Real-Time Quality Monitoring

AI enables real-time monitoring of critical quality parameters during production, ensuring that deviations from target specifications are detected immediately. Machine learning (ML) models can process vast amounts of sensor data (temperature, pressure, Flow, viscosity, etc.) from various stages of production to detect early signs of quality degradation. In chemical plants, AI can continuously analyze data streams from reactors, distillation columns, and filtration units to provide real-time feedback.

Predictive Quality Analytics

AI-powered predictive analytics allow for the forecasting of quality issues before they arise. By analyzing historical data, AI models can predict when deviations are likely to occur, enabling operators to take proactive measures. For example, machine learning models can predict when a catalyst will degrade or when a batch might not meet quality standards due to fluctuations in raw materials.

Automated Inspection and Defect Detection

AI, combined with computer vision, enables automated inspection of chemical products and packaging, improving accuracy and speed. This technology is particularly useful in identifying defects in final products, such as surface irregularities, inconsistencies in color, or dimensional faults in polymer products. AI-based vision systems analyze images of products in real time, detecting defects at a much higher speed than human inspectors.

Process Optimization for Quality

AI can optimize the entire production process to ensure consistent product quality. Using reinforcement learning. AI can adjust parameters (e.g., temperature, pressure, flow rates) in real time to improve product quality while minimizing waste. For example, in the production of high-value specialty chemicals, AI can continuously adjust conditions to optimize reaction times and improve yield, ensuring the quality of the final product.

10.4 AI in Batch Quality Control

Batch processes are common in the chemical industry, and maintaining consistent quality across batches is a challenge. AI can predict quality outcomes for each batch, analyzing past data and adjusting processing parameters in real time. By integrating AI with process control systems, manufacturers can optimize the entire batch cycle, from mixing and heating to cooling and packaging, ensuring uniformity across batches.

10.5 Digital Twins for Quality Simulation

A digital twin is a virtual model of the physical plant, which can simulate production processes, including quality control measures. AI-powered digital twins can forecast potential quality issues before they arise, simulate corrective actions, and optimize quality outcomes across the production cycle. Digital twins can also be used to run "what-if" scenarios to evaluate the impact of potential changes in the production process on product quality.

10.6 Case Examples from the Chemical Industry

Chemical Giant A: has leveraged AI in the quality control of polymer production. Using machine learning models, the company analyzes data from the production process to predict the properties of the final product and optimize the process to meet quality standards.

Chemical Giant B: has implemented AI-powered vision systems to inspect products in real time. These systems analyze images of plastic materials and packaging for defects such as cracks, color inconsistencies, or surface imperfections.

Chemical Giant C: has used AI and machine learning to monitor chemical production processes. AI-based systems predict deviations in product quality, enabling faster corrective actions, reducing waste, and improving consistency.

10.7 Challenges in Deploying AI for Quality Control

Data quality and availability: One of the main challenges in implementing AI is the quality and availability of data. For AI systems to function optimally, they need high-quality, consistent, and accurate data. Chemical plants may face issues such as missing data, noisy signals from sensors, or unstructured data from multiple sources.

Integration with existing systems: Integrating AI into legacy systems and processes can be complex. Many chemical plants rely on traditional process control and quality management systems, which may not be compatible with modern AI solutions. The integration of AI requires overcoming technical challenges, including ensuring data interoperability between legacy and AI systems.

Workforce skills and resistance to change: The introduction of AI in quality control requires employees to have a certain level of technical knowledge and adaptability. Operators and quality managers may be hesitant to trust AI-driven recommendations, especially if they are not well-versed in the technology.

High initial investment: Implementing AI technologies involves significant upfront investment in infrastructure, training, and data collection systems. Smaller companies may find these costs prohibitive, despite the long-term benefits.

Future of AI in chemical quality control: The future of AI in quality control in the chemical industry is promising, with several advancements on the horizon:

Fully autonomous quality control: As AI technologies continue to evolve, fully autonomous quality control systems could become common. These systems will autonomously monitor and adjust the production process in real time to ensure quality without human intervention.

AI-Driven sustainability: AI will help companies not only improve product quality but also minimize waste and reduce energy consumption. By optimizing processes for quality and yield, AI can contribute to more sustainable operations.

AI-Enhanced regulatory compliance: With growing regulatory pressure on the chemical industry, AI can automate compliance reporting, track quality standards, and ensure that production meets all required safety and environmental regulations.

Chapter 11 - AI in Safety for the Chemical Industry

11.1 Introduction

Safety is the backbone of the chemical industry. Given the hazardous nature of operations from handling volatile raw materials to running high-pressure, high-temperature processes ensuring safety is not just a regulatory requirement but a business imperative. Over the years, the industry has relied on safety management systems, hazard and operability studies (HAZOP), and strict compliance frameworks. However, with the rise of digital technologies, Artificial Intelligence (AI) is now transforming safety practices.

11.2 Present status of safety practices

Traditional safety systems rely heavily on reactive approaches—alarms, incident reporting, and safety audits conducted periodically. Human expertise plays a key role in hazard identification and response. While Distributed Control Systems (DCS) and Safety Instrumented Systems (SIS) provide real-time protection, they often act after a deviation has occurred. Predictive capabilities are limited, and near-misses may go unnoticed.

11.3 AI applications in safety

1. Predictive safety analytics

- AI can analyze vast amounts of process data to predict safety incidents before they occur.
- For example, machine learning models can detect early signs of runaway reactions or pressure build-ups.

Example: A big Chemical Company use DAP for trading as well as raw material. Their marketing Department purchased a cheap DAP for marketing it through their network. However they could not market it due its black in color, after few years of laying in godown some marketing employee suggested it to shift it to plant for using it as raw material. This was approved by management as they could not visualize any risk in that. The middle management were unaware about this decision, The process was producing Ammonium Nitrate in concentrated form in the melt to be prilled along with DAP for producing desired grade of Fertilizer. Process got this DAP which was having organic black coating and got mixed with Ammonium nitrate operation involve high temperature in one equipment. Some Process upset occurred during startup, after long shutdown only with DAP as P source. This upset and got process temperature higher than the normal operation zone and then runaway reaction, which was tried to controlled by normal means, which was not sufficient, resulting in big explosion in the plant, resulting in considerable damage to the plant core structure requiring considerable downtime and investment to restart the plant.

Had, plant would have implemented AI, AI would have alerted shop floor management for the ensuing risk and possible reversal of decision.

2. Hazardous Material Monitoring

- AI-enabled sensors can continuously monitor toxic gas leaks, spills, or abnormal emissions.
- Computer vision systems can detect leaks in pipelines or storage tanks through thermal imaging and drones.

3. Process Safety & Anomaly Detection

- AI algorithms can identify deviations from normal process behavior, triggering early alarms for operators.
- Reinforcement learning can optimize safety interlocks for high-risk units like reactors and distillation columns.

4. Worker Safety & Wearable AI

- Wearables equipped with AI can monitor worker fatigue, heart rate, and exposure to hazardous environments.

- Smart helmets and AR glasses can provide real-time hazard alerts.

5. Emergency Response & Simulations

- AI-powered digital twins can simulate accident scenarios, preparing operators for emergency response.
- In real time, AI can suggest optimal evacuation routes or fire-fighting strategies.

6. Regulatory Compliance Automation

- AI can automatically track compliance requirements, analyze incident reports, and prepare safety audit documentation.
- Natural Language Processing (NLP) systems can scan regulations and map them to plant operations.

11.4 Case Examples

-Chemical Giant A: Uses AI-based predictive analytics for leak detection and flare monitoring, reducing incidents.

- Chemical Giant B: Deployed AI-driven wearables to monitor worker safety in hazardous zones.
- Chemical Giant C: Experimenting with AI-based anomaly detection in refineries to enhance process safety.

11.5 Challenges in Deploying AI for Safety

1. Data Limitations

- Safety incidents are rare, making it difficult to train AI models with sufficient examples.

2. Integration with Legacy Systems

- Many plants still operate with analog or semi-digital safety systems.

3. Trust & Interpretability

- Operators may hesitate to act on AI recommendations if explanations are unclear.

4. Cost of Implementation

- High costs of AI-enabled sensors, drones, and wearables can be a barrier for smaller plants.

5. Cybersecurity

- Connecting safety systems to AI introduces new vulnerabilities.

11.6 Future of AI in Chemical Safety

- **Autonomous Safety Systems**: Plants may eventually operate with AI systems that autonomously handle emergency shutdowns.
- **Holistic safety platforms**: Integration of process, occupational, and environmental safety into a single AI-driven framework.
- Days are not far off shop floor operator's uniform of Helmet will have inbuilt camera integrated with AI system for warning any abnormal or unsafe conditions to plant management to avoid possible disruption or low efficiency operation.
- **AI + Robotics**: Robots and drones will increasingly be used for inspection in hazardous areas.
- **Green safety goals**: AI will also focus on minimizing emissions and ensuring compliance with sustainability-driven safety norms.

Chapter 12 - AI in Risk Management

12.1 Introduction: Risk as a Core Challenge in Chemical Industries

Risk management in the chemical industry is not merely a regulatory requirement—it is foundational to business continuity, safety, environmental protection, and profitability. Chemical operations handle hazardous materials, high pressures, extreme temperatures, and complex reactions prone to instability. The consequences of failure can include toxic leaks, fires, explosions, environmental disasters, regulatory penalties, and reputational damage. Traditional risk management relies heavily on historical data, expert experience, and periodic inspections, which often fail to capture real-time hazards or non-linear interdependencies between process variables.

Artificial Intelligence (AI) transforms risk management by enabling real-time monitoring, predictive risk identification, automated decision support, and continuous learning from data. AI shifts organizations from reactive risk mitigation to proactive and preventive risk strategies, reducing uncertainties in highly dynamic chemical processes.

12.2 Types of Risks in the Chemical Industry

Risk types where AI provides significant value include:

Risk Type	Typical Sources	Potential Consequences	AI Application
Operational/Process	Runaway reactions, catalyst degradation, fouling, pressure surges	Shutdown, explosion	Predictive anomaly detection

Safety (Human + Plant)	Toxic leaks, fires, manual errors	Injuries, fatalities	Computer vision, wearables
Environmental	Spills, emissions, waste leaks	Fines, contamination	Leak detection, process optimization
Compliance/Legal	Failure to meet safety standards	Penalties, shutdown	Automated documentation
Cybersecurity	IoT device breaches	Sabotage, data theft	AI-based threat monitoring
Supply/Market Risk	Shortages of hazardous raw materials	Disruption, cost spikes	Predictive forecasting

AI provides a unified platform to assess these risks holistically through data-driven models.

12.3 AI technologies transforming Risk Management

1) Predictive Analytics

- Forecasts failure probabilities based on sensor data and historical patterns
- Identifies early indicators for runaway reactions, corrosion, leak probability, and equipment degradation

2) Machine Learning (ML) for Risk scoring

- Models combine process data, safety logs, and operator behavior to continuously update dynamic risk scores

3) Computer Vision

- Detects PPE violations using cameras
- Identifies gas leaks through infrared monitoring
- Detects spills, abnormal smoke, or sparks

4) Natural Language Processing (NLP)

- Automates compliance reporting

- Extracts insights from incident reports and safety audit documents

5) Reinforcement Learning (RL)

- Suggests optimal control strategies to reduce risk during abnormal operations
- Learns safe operating windows for complex processes

6) Digital Twins

- Virtual replicas simulate hazardous scenarios without physical experimentation
- Offers predictive insights into risk response strategies such as relief valve settings or inert gas purging

12.4 AI Applications Across the Risk Lifecycle

AI supports risk management at each step:

Hazard identification

- Detects anomaly patterns, precursor signals (e.g., reactor temperature spikes)
- Recognizes unsafe behavior using CCTV plus computer vision

Risk assessment and quantification

- Dynamic risk scoring models update as conditions change
- Calculates real-time risk level of process units (e.g., distillation columns, hydrocrackers)

Risk control and mitigation

- Advises safe control actions before thresholds escalate
- Automatically adjusts feed rate, cooling, or inert gas flow

Incident response

- AI-powered emergency systems recommend evacuation routes based on leak dispersion modeling

- Drones equipped with sensors inspect hazardous zones

Audit and compliance

- Automated report generation reduces human error
- NLP analyzes new regulations and maps them to plant processes

12.5 Use cases in the Chemical Industry

1) Preventing runaway reactions

AI models predict instability by monitoring:

- Reaction temperature acceleration
- Catalyst activity drop
- Sudden gas evolution patterns
- AI triggers early alarms and may autonomously adjust cooling.

2) Toxic gas leak detection

- Infrared vision plus ML detects invisible gases
- Predictive modeling estimates dispersion and recommends operator response

3) PPE and worker behavior monitoring

- Computer vision detects missing gloves, helmets, respiratory gear
- Alerts supervisors automatically

4) AI-Driven safety in storage

AI monitors tank deformation patterns, corrosion hotspots, vent blockage, and thermal outbreathing risks.

5) Cybersecurity for smart plants

- AI continuously evaluates IoT traffic anomalies
- Prevents malicious higher-temperature control overrides

12.6 Quantifying Risk Reduction Using AI

Metric	Before AI	After AI
Leak Detection	Minutes to hours to detect	< 30 seconds with vision/IoT
Reaction Runaway Prediction	Manual inspection + alarms	Predictive forecasting (hours before event)
Worker Safety Violations	Post-incident discovery	Real-time alerts
Compliance Documentation	Manual, slow	Automated NLP documentation
Risk Scoring	Static, periodic	Continuous, real-time

AI not only reduces risk but also lowers insurance premiums, regulatory penalties, and unplanned shutdown costs.

12.7 AI Integration Framework for Risk Management

Step-by-Step Deployment

1. **Sensor and data infrastructure**

   Connect IoT devices, vision systems, gas analyzers, and SCADA.

2. **Data normalization & cybersecurity protocols**

   Ensure encrypted communication and secure networks.

3. **Model development**

   Use hybrid models (physics + ML) for hazardous processes.

4. **Digital Twin simulation and validation**

   Validate AI recommendations before plant deployment.

5. **Human-in-the-loop control**

   Operators approve AI decisions to ensure accountability.

6. **Continuous learning & regulatory updates**

   AI adapts to new regulations, materials, and operating conditions.

12.8 Challenges and Ethical Considerations

Challenge	Details	Mitigation
Data Quality	Incomplete or noisy sensor data	Redundant sensors & cleaning algorithms
Trust Issues	Operators reluctant to rely on AI	Human-in-the-loop governance
Cybersecurity	AI systems can be hacked	Firewalls + anomaly detection
Regulatory Lag	AI tech evolves faster than regulations	Collaborative standards development
Bias in Safety Models	Biased data can misjudge risks	Diverse datasets & model audits

12.9 Future Opportunities

- Predictive compliance systems that anticipate regulatory changes
- AI-enabled autonomous safety shutdowns
- GenAI systems building live risk dashboards from free-text logs
- AI-assisted emergency response robots and firefighting drones
- Blockchain + AI for transparent incident reporting
- AI will become a collaborative decision partner rather than just a tool.

Part Three

AI in Business Function.

Chapter 13 – AI in Supply Chain and Logistics for the Chemical Industry

13.1 The Complexity of Chemical Supply Chains

Chemical supply chains differ from other industries due to several inherent challenges:

High regulatory requirements: Safety, environmental, and handling rules differ by region, and compliance requires meticulous documentation (e.g., REACH, TSCA, GHS).

Specialized transport needs: Hazardous chemicals may require different kind of tankers, like refrigerated tankers for Ammonia, Dedicated Tankers for Ammonium Nitrate, inert gas blankets, or corrosion-resistant containers for Nitric Acid. Insulated tanker for Molten Sulfur.

Capital intensity: Specialized tankers, pipelines, and storage systems increase logistics costs and rigidity.

Demand and price volatility: Market dynamics, geopolitical events, and seasonal variations significantly affect both supply and demand.

• **Multi-tiered supply structures**: Raw materials, intermediates, and final products pass through several processing and transformation stages across continents. For example loading from Storage silo at source location to finally unloading to storage silo at destination location and further feeding operation to feed bins.

Most chemical firms operate ERP systems (SAP, Oracle, etc.), along with transport and warehouse management systems. However, the degree of digital integration may varies: some firms currently rely heavily on spreadsheets, while digital leaders employ predictive and prescriptive analytics for dynamic decision-making.

13.2 AI Capabilities in Supply Chain and Logistics

AI applications span across the supply chain, offering data-driven insights and automation in areas such as:

1. Demand forecasting

Machine learning integrates sales history, market trends, and even weather data to predict demand variations. For example, fertilizer producers can forecast regional demand using crop sowing patterns and monsoon forecasts.

2. Inventory optimization

AI algorithms balance carrying costs with service levels, optimizing stock levels across multiple warehouses and plants. Reinforcement learning helps simulate different stocking policies based on lead times, safety stock needs, and shelf-life constraints.

3. Production scheduling

AI synchronizes production runs with forecasted demand, raw material arrivals, and maintenance schedules—reducing idle time and improving throughput.

4. Transportation and routing optimization

AI dynamically re-routes shipments considering traffic, weather, port congestion or geopolitical situations. For hazardous materials, it optimizes routes for both cost and safety, ensuring compliance with local transport laws.

5. Warehouse automation and handling

Computer vision and robotics enhance safety and efficiency in warehouses. AI monitors temperature, humidity, and gas levels to maintain compliance and prevent incidents.

6. Trade compliance and documentation

NLP tools automate the generation of Safety Data Sheets (SDS), classification under HS codes, and export documentation, minimizing customs delays and errors.

7. Supplier Risk Management

AI analyzes financial data, ESG performance, geopolitical exposure, and historical reliability to assess supplier risk, enabling proactive mitigation.

8. Sustainability and Carbon Tracking

AI models estimate emissions from transportation and suggest optimizations such as modal shifts or better utilization of return loads to reduce carbon footprint.

13.3 Data Foundations for AI Models

AI performance depends heavily on data integration from multiple sources, including:

- ERP & MES Systems: Orders, schedules, inventory data.
- Transportation Management Systems (TMS): Route and carrier performance.
- External Feeds: Commodity prices, weather, geopolitical updates.
- IoT Sensors: Real-time data from transport vehicles and containers.
- Blockchain Systems: Ensuring traceability and tamper-proof transactions.

Data quality, consistency, and accessibility are critical success factors for deploying AI across supply chains.

13.4 Benefits of AI in Chemical Supply Chains

The measurable benefits of AI adoption include:

• Higher Forecast Accuracy – Reduced stockouts and overproduction.

• Lower Logistics Costs – Optimized routes and container utilization.

• Faster Response to Disruptions – AI detects risks early and proposes alternatives instantly.

• Improved Customer Satisfaction – Enhanced delivery reliability and product availability.

• Sustainability Gains – Reduced waste, optimized fuel use, and better environmental performance.

13.5 Implementation Challenges

Despite its promise, AI deployment faces practical obstacles:

Data Challenges – Fragmented data across ERP, TMS, and spreadsheets; poor-quality inputs; limited real-time visibility.

Organizational Resistance – Reluctance to trust AI recommendations; lack of training for supply chain personnel.

Technology Integration – Compatibility with legacy ERP systems and cybersecurity threats.

Regulatory Compliance – Ensuring AI-driven decisions meet hazardous material transport and safety standards.

13.6 Case Studies and Industry Examples

• Bulk Liquid Logistics: A global petrochemical firm used AI for tanker scheduling and port congestion management, reducing demurrage costs by 15%.

• Fertilizer Distribution: AI forecasting based on weather and crop data improved rural inventory placement and minimized stock imbalances.

• Specialty Chemicals: AI optimized small-batch campaign scheduling, reducing lead times and improving customer responsiveness.

13.7 Future of AI-Driven Supply Chains

Emerging technologies point toward self-learning, autonomous supply chains characterized by:

1. Digital Twins – Simulating supply chain operations end-to-end for scenario testing (e.g., port closures, supplier defaults).

2. Autonomous Logistics – AI-coordinated autonomous trucks, drones, and robotic warehouses operating in controlled chemical zones.

3. Blockchain and AI Integration – Enhancing transparency, traceability, and fraud detection across international trade networks.

4. Circular and Sustainable Supply Chains – AI-optimized reverse logistics for recycling solvents, plastics, and catalysts.

5. Predictive Risk Management – Continuous monitoring of geopolitical, weather, and supplier risk with automated mitigation.

13.8 Implementation Roadmap for Chemical Firms

Phase 1: Foundation – Consolidate data sources and define governance structures.

Phase 2: Pilot Projects – Run small-scale AI pilots for forecasting or routing optimization.

Phase 3: Scale-up – Integrate AI into global operations and establish an AI Center of Excellence.

Phase 4: Transformation – Move toward autonomous, sustainable, and circular AI-driven supply chains.

Chapter 14 - Artificial Intelligence in Procurement for the Chemical Industry

14.1 Introduction

Procurement is the backbone of the chemical industry, ensuring uninterrupted operations by securing raw materials, equipment, services, and logistics at the right time, cost, and quality. Given the global scale of the industry, procurement decisions often span multiple geographies, involve complex supplier networks, and require adherence to strict environmental, safety, and compliance standards. The volatile nature of commodity markets, fluctuating energy prices, geopolitical risks, and sustainability. Artificial Intelligence (AI) offers transformative potential in reshaping procurement. It enables procurement professionals to shift from transactional activities to strategic decision-making. AI not only enhances efficiency and reduces costs but also helps predict risks, optimize supplier collaboration, and ensure sustainability. This chapter explores the current state of AI adoption in procurement in the chemical industry, benefits, challenges, case studies, and future pathways.

14.2Strategic Role of Procurement in the Chemical Industry

Procurement in the chemical sector is far more than the simple act of purchasing goods and services. It is a highly strategic function that directly impacts profitability, sustainability, and competitiveness. Some critical aspects of procurement include:

- Raw Material Dependence: Chemical production relies heavily on petroleum-based feedstocks, natural gas, catalysts, Liquid and Solid high volume raw material and specialty additives. Prices for these inputs fluctuate widely based on crude oil prices, supply-demand imbalances, and geopolitical events.

- Capital-Intensive Equipment: Equipment such as distillation columns, reactors, and specialized pumps requires careful sourcing with long lead times and high quality standards.
- Regulatory Compliance: Procurement must ensure that materials meet stringent EHS standards, REACH regulations and other global and local compliance frameworks.
- Supplier Ecosystem: Procurement teams must maintain relationships with suppliers across continents, balancing cost, quality, and reliability.

The importance of procurement is heightened in the chemical sector because any disruption—whether raw material shortages, supplier bankruptcy, or regulatory non-compliance—can cause significant production and financial losses.

14.3 Evolution of Procurement in the Chemical Industry

Procurement has evolved from a transactional function focused on purchase orders to a strategic discipline. Traditionally, procurement teams relied on human negotiation, historical data, and supplier relationships. With globalization and digitalization, procurement functions now require advanced tools. ERP systems like SAP and Oracle enabled digital procurement processes, but AI takes this further by enabling predictive insights, automation, and risk forecasting.

In the chemical industry, AI is enabling a paradigm shift from reactive to proactive procurement. Instead of waiting for disruptions, AI helps anticipate problems and recommend corrective measures in advance.

14.4 Current Status of AI Adoption in Procurement

AI adoption in procurement varies widely among chemical companies. Large global players such as CHEMICAL GIANT A are experimenting with AI-powered procurement platforms, while smaller firms remain cautious due to budgetary constraints. Areas where AI is currently being applied include:

- Spend Analytics: Identifying patterns in procurement expenditure and uncovering savings opportunities.
- Supplier Selection and Risk Scoring: Using machine learning algorithms to evaluate suppliers based on quality, delivery performance, financial stability, and ESG compliance.
- Contract Management: NLP-driven platforms that review thousands of supplier contracts to flag risks and compliance issues.
- Demand Forecasting: Predicting material needs using AI-powered predictive analytics.
- Automation of Routine Tasks: Using Robotic Process Automation to automate invoice matching, purchase order creation, and approvals.
- Fraud Detection: Machine learning models identifying anomalies in transaction patterns.

Despite progress, adoption is still at an early stage. Many organizations use AI only for pilot projects rather than full-scale deployment.

14.5 AI Technologies Transforming Procurement

Several AI technologies drive the transformation of procurement

- Machine Learning (ML): Enables predictive analytics for demand, pricing, and supplier performance.
- Natural Language Processing (NLP): Helps interpret unstructured data from contracts, emails, and regulatory documents.
- Robotic Process Automation (RPA): Automates repetitive tasks to free procurement professionals for strategic work.
- Predictive Analytics: Anticipates risks such as supplier default, demand surges, and commodity price spikes.

- Computer Vision: Supports material quality verification by analyzing supplier-provided images or scanned documents.
- Blockchain + AI: Improves trust and transparency in procurement transactions.

14.6 Benefits of AI in Procurement for the Chemical Industry

AI offers significant advantages to procurement teams, including:

- Cost Reduction: Identifying cost-saving opportunities and supporting effective supplier negotiations.
- Efficiency Gains: Automating manual tasks reduces cycle time for procurement processes.
- Risk Management: Identifying supplier-related risks early.
- Compliance: Ensuring adherence to EHS and global regulatory standards.
- Sustainability: Supporting ESG goals by selecting environmentally responsible suppliers.
- AI can reduce frauds by masking vendor details from the offer submitted by them,
- Strategic Value Creation: Shifting procurement from a tactical to a strategic function.

14.7 Detailed Use Cases of AI in Chemical Procurement

a. Raw Material Sourcing and Price Forecasting AI models analyze global commodity prices, shipping routes, weather conditions, and geopolitical developments to predict raw material price trends. For example, anticipating fluctuations in naphtha or ethylene prices helps optimize procurement contracts.

b. Supplier Relationship Management AI-based dashboards track supplier performance on delivery timelines, defect rates, and sustainability scores. This enables proactive supplier management and strengthens long-term partnerships.

c. Contract Analysis and Lifecycle Management AI-driven NLP systems scan thousands of contracts to identify risks, non-standard clauses, and compliance gaps. They also help consolidate contracts to reduce supplier fragmentation.

d. Inventory Optimization Balancing cost and availability is critical in chemicals, where storage costs for hazardous materials can be high and it is also limited to tank capacity. AI models forecast demand and recommend optimal inventory levels.

e. Fraud and Anomaly Detection Procurement fraud, such as duplicate invoicing or collusion, is detected by AI systems analyzing transactional anomalies.

f. Sustainable Procurement AI ensures procurement aligns with green initiatives, such as sourcing bio-based feedstocks or low-carbon energy inputs.

14.8Possible implementation of AI in Procurement Department.

Procurement department can be automated with entire cycle of procurement starting generation of requirement to placement of order, delivery, inspection and Final payment.

- AI can predict requirement of General items.
- AI Can help in writing specification and Bill of quantity
- AI can help in finalizing technical terms & NIT conditions
- AI can help in finalizing commercial terms & NIT conditions
- AI can help in finalizing Shipping terms & NIT conditions
- AI can help in finalizing inspection terms & NIT conditions
- AI can help in finalizing Tender document.
- AI can help in Finalizing vendor prequalification criteria and ensure enough competition in the Tender in following scenario
    a) When abundant vendors are available.

b) When just sufficient vendors are available.
c) When vendors are scares to find.

- AI can help finalizing Vendor list who may bid for the job.
- AI can grade Vendors based on criteria of delivery risk, Quality risk and financial risk.
- AI can get vendor's capability feedback
- AI can help in floating Tenders to Bidders either on limited tender basis, prequalified bidder or to press advertisement or through Website.
- AI can help in evaluating technical bid
- AI can help in making technical comparative statement
- AI can help in making technical Queries for deviation quoted by the bidders, for reconfirming the offer in conformity to technical requirement and specifications.
- AI can help in preparing loading criteria for acceptable deviation in technical and commercial conditions.
- AI can help in preparing approval note for opening commercial offer of technically acceptable bidders and rejecting non acceptable offer
- AI can help in evaluating commercial bid
- AI can help in making commercial comparative statement
- AI can help in making commercial Queries for deviation quoted by the bidders, for reconfirming the offer in conformity to Commercial conditions.
- AI can help in preparing approval notes for placement of order.
- AI can help in drafting LOI and purchase order.
- AI can help raising alerts for inspection for stagewise inspection or final inspection before dispatch or after delivery as the case may be.
- AI can help in reducing time line for release of payment raise alerts for each mile stone delayed and hence reduce delay in release of payments, if required.

- AI can reduce frauds by masking vendor details from offer before evauation

14.9Challenges in AI Adoption

AI adoption is not without hurdles:

- Data Quality: Poor data quality limits AI effectiveness.
- Change Resistance: Procurement staff may fear displacement by AI.
- Cost of Implementation: High upfront costs deter smaller players.
- Supplier Transparency: Limited access to supplier data reduces AI model accuracy.
- Ethical Concerns: Bias in AI models may lead to unfair supplier selection.
- Cybersecurity Risks: Digital platforms face risks of hacking and fraud.

14.10 Future Outlook of AI in Procurement

The next decade will see procurement evolve into a fully AI-enabled strategic function. Trends include:

- End-to-End Autonomous Procurement: From requisition to payment with minimal human intervention.
- Cognitive Procurement: AI systems learning from data to improve continuously.
- AI and Blockchain Integration: Transparent, traceable, fraud-proof procurement.
- Real-Time Decision Making: AI-driven procurement decisions in real time based on global data inputs.
- ESG-Driven Procurement: AI ensuring that suppliers align with sustainability goals.

14.11 Case Studies in the Chemical Industry

Case Study 1: Chemical Giant A uses AI for supplier risk analysis and spend analytics, generating millions in savings.

Case Study 2: Chemical Giant B deploys NLP for contract analysis, reducing cycle times significantly.

Case Study 3: Chemical Giant C implements AI for raw material price forecasting, improving negotiation outcomes.

14.12 Roadmap for Implementing AI in Procurement

Step 1: Assess procurement maturity and data readiness.

Step 2: Start with pilot projects in high-value areas.

Step 3: Scale AI by integrating with ERP and procurement systems.

Step 4: Build internal AI capabilities and train procurement teams.

Step 5: Continuously monitor and refine AI systems.

Chapter 15 - AI in Store Department in chemical Industry

15.1 Current status

Under current Computerized data is exiting under SAP or ERP for Store system

All store item is codified

Item owner is identified.

Duplicate codified items are those items which has been codified twice on different occasion.

These are identified manually with help of computer.

New items are received and inspection carried out before stock charge.

Availability of Item is available location wise.

- Central Store
- Plant Store
- Store of other units.

Item are identified as obsolete or slow moving or nonmoving items manually.

Some General items are procured on rate contract items.

Scrape are also stored in store.

Scrape item and obsolete items are sold time to time.

15.2 AI can further improved Store Department

All items having one specification should have single code. AI can detect this and unify the code

Flexible or multiple Item owners can be prepared by AI.

AI can detect duplication of material code from description and specification hence merged the codes, so that all duplicate codes are eliminated.

AI can generate alert to Owner, as soon as any item's delivery is received for immediate inspection before stock charged and usage.

AI can help in better availability of parts once a requirement is searched not only by item code, but also with description and specification. AI can also give availability of lower specification material if there is urgency for usage.

AI is better capable to predicting consumption general items during a period and arrange delivery of the same through rate contract suppliers.

AI can give report on better utilization of obsolete and scrape items usage.

Chapter 16 - AI in Marketing Chemical Products

16.1 Introduction

The chemical industry, being one of the largest and most diversified sectors in the world, is highly competitive and globalized. Marketing of chemical products presents unique challenges due to the complexity of product portfolios, regulatory requirements, technical specifications, specialized transportation and storage infrastructure and a customer base that ranges from individual manufacturers to multinational corporations. In this context, Artificial Intelligence (AI) is emerging as a transformative tool that enables companies to market their products more efficiently, personalize customer engagement, optimize pricing strategies, and predict market trends with greater accuracy.

This chapter explores how AI is revolutionizing marketing in the chemical industry. It covers the role of AI in customer insights, demand forecasting, product positioning, digital marketing, pricing optimization, supply chain integration, and customer relationship management. By analyzing real-world applications and future possibilities, the chapter highlights the strategic importance of AI in creating sustainable competitive advantage in chemical product marketing.

16.2 Unique Challenges of Marketing Chemical Products

Marketing chemical products is inherently more complex compared to other industries. Some of the key challenges include:

1. Technical Complexity of Products – Chemicals are not generic commodities; each product comes with detailed specifications, safety data sheets, and technical parameters that customers must evaluate carefully before purchase.

2. Regulatory Compliance – Stringent environmental, health, and safety regulations govern chemical production, distribution, and use. Marketing strategies must ensure compliance with these standards while still promoting the product's value.

3. Diverse Customer Base – Customers range from pharmaceutical companies to construction firms, each with different needs, purchase cycles, Different Quality, Highly different pricing vary several times for same product with different quality and expectations.

4. Long Sales Cycles – Unlike fast-moving consumer goods, chemical sales cycles are long, involving detailed evaluation, product trials, and negotiations.

5. Transportation and Storage Infrastructure – Chemicals require special and different storage and transportation infrastructure, which cannot be created overnight. Most of the times storage system is owned by either party and transportation infrastructure is used by outsourcing.

For example for transportation of Ammonia refrigerated tanker are required, for Nitric Acid SS-304 tankers are required, for AN melt dedicated tanker is must, while sulfuric acid(99%) and Methanol MS Tankers are required both having different Specification, for molten sulfur insulated tankers are required.

6. Global Competition – The industry is global, and companies must compete on innovation, quality, price, and service while managing cross-border complexities, only prohibited by high transportation cost.

16.3 AI in Marketing: An Overview

Artificial Intelligence offers solutions to many of these challenges by enabling smarter, data-driven decision-making. Some of the key applications include:

- Customer Segmentation – AI algorithms analyze purchasing data, industry trends, and customer behavior to segment customers more effectively. Incase if you are able to move your product to different segment with some improvement in quality can lead to several time price realization.

For Example: Calcium Carbonate available in Fertilizer plant is of low quality and as it is can be used only for making Black bord chalk manufacturing.

If they are able to make this product superior by reducing impurities it can be used by Paper Industry, which can increase price realization of same product by 10 times of chalk Industry. Even in paper industry price will depends upon whiteness of product.

Same product with further strict purity, is also having demand in pharmaceutical Industry where price realization is 10 times of paper industry demand.

- Predictive Analytics – Machine learning models forecast demand, market growth, and product adoption trends.
- Personalized Marketing – AI enables customized campaigns targeting specific industries, regions, or even individual clients.
- Pricing Optimization – Dynamic pricing models use real-time data to adjust prices according to demand, competition, and raw material costs and
- Chatbots and Virtual Assistants – AI-driven tools enhance customer engagement by providing 24/7 support and technical guidance.

16.4 Customer Insights through AI

Understanding customer behavior and preferences is crucial in the chemical industry. Traditional methods such as surveys and sales reports are insufficient for capturing complex customer patterns. AI provides a deeper understanding through:

Data Integration – Combining internal sales data with external sources like market reports, industry news, and regulatory updates.

Sentiment Analysis – Using natural language processing (NLP) to analyze customer feedback, online forums, and social media for insights on brand perception and emerging needs.

Behavioral Prediction – Identifying potential buyers based on previous interactions, purchase history, and engagement patterns.

For example, a chemical company selling polymers may use AI tools to predict which automobile manufacturers are most likely to increase orders based on vehicle production trends, fuel economy regulations, and sustainability goals.

16.5 Demand Forecasting and Market Trend Analysis

One of the most critical aspects of chemical product marketing is accurate demand forecasting. AI enhances forecasting models by incorporating:

1. Historical Sales Data – Machine learning algorithms analyze past sales patterns to predict future demand more accurately.

2. External Factors – AI incorporates macroeconomic indicators, raw material price fluctuations, and industry growth forecasts into predictive models.

3. Scenario Planning – Advanced AI models simulate multiple scenarios such as regulatory changes, trade tariffs, or environmental policies to estimate their impact on demand.

This allows companies to align production schedules, marketing strategies, and inventory planning with anticipated market needs, thereby minimizing risks and maximizing opportunities.

16.6 AI-Driven Product Positioning

Positioning a chemical product in the market requires differentiation strategies. AI contributes to this by:

Competitive Analysis – Monitoring competitor activities, pricing strategies, and product launches in real-time.

Market Gap Identification – Detecting underserved customer segments or unmet needs where a new product can be positioned effectively.

Substitute identification - detecting substitute availability of product may pose a threat. AI can detect early warning to take corrective actions.

Sustainability Insights – Identifying markets where sustainability and green chemistry are major differentiators, enabling targeted marketing campaigns.

16.7 Digital Marketing and AI Tools

With increasing digitalization, AI is also transforming how chemical companies use digital channels for marketing:

1. Programmatic Advertising – AI algorithms automatically purchase digital ad spaces, targeting the right audience with precision.

2. Search Engine Optimization (SEO) – AI-powered SEO tools optimize content to ensure chemical products are visible in industry-specific searches.

3. Content Personalization – Websites and online portals adapt content dynamically based on visitor profiles, offering customized product recommendations and technical documents.

4. Chatbots and Virtual Agents – Providing real-time support for technical queries, product documentation, and order tracking.

For instance, a specialty chemicals company may use AI to recommend the best adhesive product to an electronics manufacturer by analyzing their previous purchases and current production requirements.

16.8 Pricing Optimization with AI

Pricing in the chemical industry is highly dynamic due to volatility in raw material costs, demand fluctuations, and currency exchange rates. AI-powered pricing models allow companies to:

- Analyze competitor pricing and customer sensitivity in real-time and cost to customer including transportation cost or any other penalty cost due to poor quality of product.
- Adjust prices dynamically to maximize revenue while maintaining competitiveness.
- Forecast the impact of raw material cost changes on final product pricing.
- Provide tailored quotations for large industrial clients, improving negotiation outcomes.

16.9 Supply Chain and Marketing Integration

Marketing in the chemical industry is closely linked to supply chain performance. AI enables integration by:

- Forecasting raw material requirements based on market demand.
- Optimizing logistics for timely delivery of chemical products.
- Reducing stockouts and ensuring availability of key products in target markets.

16.10 Customer Relationship Management (CRM)

AI-enhanced CRM systems are particularly valuable in chemical product marketing. They help companies:

- Prioritize leads based on predictive scoring models.
- Track customer interactions and provide personalized communication.
- Automate follow-ups and reminders for long sales cycles.
- Improve customer retention through proactive service and support.

16.11 Case Studies

1. Chemical Giant A – Uses AI tools for demand forecasting and supply chain optimization, improving product availability for customers worldwide.

2. Chemical Giant B – Implements AI-driven pricing models to adjust quotes dynamically based on customer profiles and market conditions.
3. Chemical Giant C – Employs AI-powered digital platforms to offer customized solutions to clients in specialty chemical segments.

16.12 Future Outlook: AI in Chemical Product Marketing

As AI continues to advance, future marketing strategies in the chemical industry will be characterized by:

- Hyper-Personalization – Delivering customized marketing messages and product offerings at an individual client level.
- Predictive Customer Engagement – Anticipating customer needs before they explicitly arise, thereby shortening sales cycles.
- Integration with Sustainability Goals – AI helping companies align product marketing with global sustainability targets and ESG (Environmental, Social, Governance) requirements.
- Immersive Experiences – Use of AI in virtual reality (VR) and augmented reality (AR) to demonstrate chemical applications to clients.

Chapter 17 - AI in Finance Department of a Chemical Company

17.1 Introduction

The finance department plays a central role in the operations of any chemical company. From managing budgets and controlling costs to evaluating investments, monitoring compliance, and ensuring liquidity, the finance function is crucial in driving growth and profitability. In the chemical industry—characterized by high capital intensity, global supply chains, fluctuating raw material prices, and complex regulations—finance leaders face challenges that demand both agility and precision.

Artificial Intelligence (AI) is increasingly emerging as a transformative enabler in finance. By leveraging AI, chemical companies can improve financial forecasting, enhance risk management, optimize working capital, streamline compliance processes, and strengthen decision-making. This chapter explores in depth how AI can be deployed in the finance department of a chemical company to create efficiency, transparency, and value.

Finance Department is having following main function in the industry

- Planning of cashflow, Working Capital, receipt of marketing proceeds.
- Payment system
- Budgeting for expenditure
- Payroll
- Concurring procurement
- Costing
- Taxation (Mod vat, Employee Income Tax, Corporate Tax)
- Predicting Return on Investment

- Help top management in deciding production scheduling based on profit/contribution to company at regular interval.
- Capital Investment Decision
- Merger & Acquisition Decision
- Insurance and Risk mitigation.
- Auditing
- Reporting
- Statutory compliance

17.2 Unique Financial Challenges in the Chemical Industry

The chemical industry has specific financial challenges that differentiate it from other sectors:

1. High Capital Investments – Chemical plants require massive capital investments in infrastructure, machinery, and technology, making financial planning critical.

2. Volatile Raw Material Costs – Prices of all feedstocks and other raw materials fluctuate significantly, impacting profitability.

3. Global Operations – Many chemical companies operate across multiple geographies, leading to complexities in taxation, currency exchange, and compliance.

4. Long Payback Periods – Large projects have long gestation periods, requiring robust financial modeling to ensure viability.

5. Regulatory Environment – Compliance with environmental, health, and safety regulations creates additional financial burdens and requires meticulous reporting.

17.3 AI in Financial Forecasting and Planning

Forecasting in the chemical industry involves predicting sales, costs, raw material prices, and capital expenditure requirements. Traditional forecasting methods often fail to capture the complexity and volatility of this industry. AI-driven forecasting models improve accuracy through:

- Predictive Analytics – Machine learning models analyze historical data, macroeconomic indicators, raw material prices, and market demand to generate accurate forecasts.
- Scenario Analysis – AI simulates multiple scenarios (e.g., changes in crude oil prices, new regulations, or currency fluctuations) to assess financial implications.
- Automated Forecast Updates – AI systems continuously update financial forecasts in real-time as new data becomes available.

For example, an AI tool can forecast the impact of rising crude oil prices on polyethylene production costs, or rise in phosphoric acid price or rock phosphate cost on Fertilizer production cost, enabling finance teams to adjust budgets and pricing strategies accordingly.

17.4 AI in Budgeting and Cost Control

Budgeting is often a tedious process in chemical companies due to the diversity of products and global operations. AI enhances budgeting by:

- Automating Data Collection – Gathering financial and operational data from multiple sources in real-time. For example after placement of order and its payment schedule AI can easily predict cash outflow in real time.
- Variance Analysis – Identifying deviations between budgeted and actual costs more quickly and accurately.
- Cost Optimization – AI identifies cost drivers, inefficiencies, and opportunities for savings in production, logistics, and procurement.

AI-powered systems not only speed up budgeting but also provide more dynamic, flexible budgets that adapt to changing business conditions.

17.5 Risk Management and AI

The chemical industry faces multiple risks, including commodity price volatility, currency fluctuations, credit risks, and regulatory changes. AI supports risk management through:

- Credit Risk Assessment – Using AI to evaluate customer payment histories, financial statements, and market data to predict creditworthiness.
- Insurance Policy – Use AI to identify the machinery and equipment risk and guide the insurance team of the company for appropriate insurance cover for breakdown or loss of profit.
- Fraud Detection – Machine learning algorithms detect unusual financial transactions and anomalies, helping prevent fraud.
- Market Risk Modeling – AI-driven simulations model the financial impact of raw material price volatility or supply chain disruptions.
- Regulatory Compliance Risk – NLP-based systems scan regulatory updates and ensure compliance with financial reporting standards.

17.6 Cash Flow and Working Capital Optimization

Maintaining healthy cash flow and working capital is essential for chemical companies due to their capital-intensive nature. AI tools help finance departments:

- Accounts Receivable Optimization – Predicting which clients are likely to delay payments and suggesting proactive collection strategies.
- Inventory Management – Integrating with supply chain AI systems to align working capital with production schedules and market demand.
- Payables Management – Optimizing payment schedules to suppliers without straining relationships or disrupting supply chains.

For instance, AI-driven working capital optimization can reduce days sales outstanding (DSO) by predicting late payments and recommending follow-up actions.

17.7 AI in Investment Appraisal and Capital Allocation

Evaluating new projects—whether a new plant, product line, or acquisition—is critical for long-term profitability. AI enhances investment appraisal by:

- Dynamic Financial Modeling – Continuously updating project feasibility models with real-time data on costs, revenues, and risks.
- Scenario-Based Valuation – Estimating project returns under multiple possible futures, such as regulatory changes or demand shifts.
- Portfolio Optimization – AI identifies the optimal allocation of capital across projects to maximize returns while managing risks.

17.8 Compliance and Regulatory Reporting with AI

The finance department must ensure compliance with local and international accounting standards, taxation rules, and industry-specific regulations. AI streamlines compliance by:

- Automating Tax Compliance – AI systems monitor global tax regulations and ensure adherence.
- Financial Reporting – Natural language generation (NLG) tools prepare financial reports automatically, reducing errors and human effort.
- Audit Readiness – AI flags discrepancies and ensures all transactions are traceable for audits.

17.9 AI in Financial Decision Support

AI also assists CFOs and finance managers in strategic decision-making by providing actionable insights. Examples include:

- Profitability Analysis – AI analyzes margins at a granular level (by product, region, or customer) to identify areas of improvement.
- Capital Structuring – Machine learning models recommend optimal debt-to-equity ratios based on interest rates, cash flow, and risk profiles.
- Strategic Planning – AI identifies long-term growth opportunities, such as expanding into new markets or product diversification.

17.10 Case Studies

1. Chemical Giant A – Uses AI for real-time financial forecasting and global cost control, improving decision-making at the corporate level.

2. Chemical Giant B – Employs AI-driven risk models to hedge against raw material and currency risks.

3. Chemical Giant C – Implements AI-powered working capital management systems that optimize receivables and payables, improving liquidity.

17.11 Future Outlook: AI in Chemical Finance

Looking ahead, AI in the finance department of chemical companies will evolve in several key directions:

- Autonomous Finance Systems – Finance processes such as forecasting, budgeting, and reporting will become increasingly automated, requiring minimal human intervention.
- Integration with ESG Metrics – AI will help finance departments track and report environmental, social, and governance (ESG) performance, aligning financial strategies with sustainability goals.
- Blockchain and AI Synergy – Blockchain integration will provide transparency in transactions, while AI will enhance risk detection and compliance.
- Advanced Predictive Capabilities – Future AI systems will not just analyze historical data but also anticipate disruptions before they occur, allowing proactive financial strategies.

Chapter 18 - AI in the HR Department of the Chemical Industry

18.1 Introduction

Human Resources (HR) functions as the backbone of every organization, ensuring the right people, skills, and culture are in place to drive success. In the chemical industry—where safety, compliance, technical expertise, and workforce stability are critical—the HR department plays a strategic role far beyond recruitment and payroll. From ensuring safety-conscious hiring to building leadership pipelines, managing diversity, and aligning workforce strategies with long-term sustainability goals, HR departments in chemical companies must constantly evolve to meet new challenges.

The advent of Artificial Intelligence (AI) has fundamentally reshaped the HR function. Once limited to administrative tasks, HR is now a strategic partner powered by advanced technologies. AI offers the ability to analyze vast volumes of workforce data, identify hidden trends, enhance decision-making, and automate repetitive tasks, freeing HR professionals to focus on higher-value strategic work.

This chapter explores in detail how AI is transforming the HR department within the chemical industry. We will examine its role in recruitment, training and development, performance management, employee engagement, compliance, health and safety, diversity, and workforce planning. Along the way, we will discuss case studies, benefits, challenges, and the future outlook for AI in HR.

The Role of HR in the Chemical Industry

The HR function in chemical companies carries unique responsibilities:

2. Recruitment of Specialized Talent – Engineers, process technologists, safety officers, R&D scientists, and plant operators.
3. Workforce Safety and Compliance – Ensuring compliance with labor laws, environmental regulations, and strict OHS guidelines.
4. Skill Development and Continuous Learning – Training on hazardous chemicals, safety protocols, and emerging technologies.
5. Performance Management and Productivity – Monitoring KPIs and aligning workforce performance with production targets.
6. Employee Engagement and Retention – Reducing attrition in high-stress environments.
7. 6. Diversity and Inclusion – Encouraging gender diversity and inclusiveness in a male- dominated industry.

These functions are highly data-driven, making them ripe for AI integration.

18.2 Applications of AI in HR Departments

1. AI in Recruitment and Talent Acquisition

- Smart Candidate Sourcing
- Resume Screening
- Bias Reduction
- Chatbots for Candidate Engagement
- Predictive Hiring

2. AI in Training and Development

- Personalized Learning Pathways
- VR + AI for Safety Training
- Adaptive Learning Platforms
- Knowledge Retention
- Upskilling for Digital Transformation

3. AI in Performance Management

- Continuous Monitoring
- 360-Degree Feedback Analysis
- Predictive Performance Modeling
- Well-Being Tracking

4. AI in Payroll and Workforce Administration

- Automated Payroll Processing
- Fraud Detection
- Benefits Optimization

5. AI in Employee Engagement and Retention

- Sentiment Analysis
- Engagement Chatbots
- Attrition Prediction
- Customized Engagement Programs

6. AI in Compliance and Safety

- Regulatory Compliance Monitoring
- Occupational Safety Monitoring
- Incident Prediction

7. AI in Diversity, Equity, and Inclusion

- Bias-Free Recruitment
- Diversity Analytics
- Inclusive Training Recommendations

8. AI in Strategic Workforce Planning

- Manpower Forecasting
- Succession Planning
- Gig and Contract Workforce Optimization

18.3 Benefits of AI in HR for Chemical Industry

1. Faster Recruitment – Shortens hiring cycle time.
2. Improved Safety – AI-powered safety training and monitoring reduce incidents.
3. Improved Training – AI Power training schedule to increase the performance of employee and their skill.
4. Reduced Attrition – Predictive analytics help retain talent.
5. Cost Efficiency – Automation reduces administrative overhead.
6. Better Compliance – AI ensures legal and regulatory alignment.
7. Enhanced Diversity – Data-driven approaches promote fairness.

18.4 Challenges and Limitations

- Data Privacy Concerns – Employee data must be safeguarded.
- Algorithm Bias – Poorly designed AI models may perpetuate bias.
- Integration Issues – Legacy HR systems may not support AI.
- Resistance to Change – Employees may fear displacement.
- Cost of Implementation – AI adoption requires investment.

Case Studies

Case Study 1: Recruitment at a Global Chemical Company – AI reduced time-to-hire by 40%.

Case Study 2: Safety Training in a Fertilizer Plant – VR+AI reduced incidents by 50%.

Case Study 3: Attrition Prediction at a Petrochemical Company – Targeted engagement reduced turnover by 20%.

18.5 Future Outlook

- AI-Enabled Employee Digital Twins
- AI + Robotics in HR
- Emotion AI for mood tracking
- Blockchain + AI for secure HR
- AI-Powered Sustainability Metrics

Chapter 19 – Ethics, Safety, and Regulatory Compliance in AI for the Chemical Industry

Artificial Intelligence can deliver huge gains in efficiency, quality, and innovation — but in the chemical sector, a single wrong decision can have serious safety, environmental, or legal consequences.

AI must therefore be developed, deployed, and monitored with ethics, safety, and regulatory compliance as core principles.

19.1 The High-Stakes Nature of Chemicals

Unlike some industries, errors in chemical processes can lead to:

Safety incidents (explosions, toxic leaks, fires).

Environmental damage (contamination, emissions violations).

Regulatory penalties (fines, license revocation, shutdowns).

This reality means AI must meet the same or higher reliability standards as traditional control systems.

19.2 Ethical Principles for AI in Chemicals

The chemical industry can borrow from established AI ethics frameworks, but must adapt them for its context:

Safety First

AI must never compromise process safety limits.

Fail-safe defaults should activate if predictions are uncertain.

Transparency and Explainability

Models should provide interpretable outputs so engineers understand why a recommendation is made.

Black-box predictions in safety-critical operations should be avoided.

Fairness and Bias Avoidance

Ensure datasets do not contain biases that could affect decision-making (e.g., supplier selection, quality grading).

Accountability

Always define who is responsible for AI decisions — the algorithm or the human operator.

19.3 Regulatory Frameworks Affecting AI in Chemicals

Several existing regulations indirectly govern AI in chemical plants:

Process Safety Management (PSM) – OSHA standards in the U.S.

REACH and CLP – EU chemical safety and labeling laws.

ISO 9001 & ISO 14001 – Quality and environmental management systems.

Cybersecurity regulations for industrial control systems (e.g., IEC 62443).

AI may also face upcoming AI-specific laws, such as:

EU AI Act – Classifies AI in high-risk industries with strict transparency and testing requirements.

Industry-specific safety certification for AI-driven process control systems.

19.4 Safety in AI Deployment

Before AI is implemented in production:

Hazard and operability (HAZOP) review of AI use cases.

Simulation testing under normal, extreme, and failure conditions.

Human-in-the-loop control for critical operations until AI proves long-term stability.

19.5 Data Privacy and Intellectual Property (IP)

In R&D and product development:

AI may process proprietary formulations and process parameters — these must be protected with encryption and secure storage.

Collaborative AI projects should have clear IP ownership clauses to avoid disputes.

19.6 Cybersecurity Risks

As AI often connects to plant control systems:

Use network segmentation to separate AI systems from core control layers.

Conduct penetration testing to prevent hacking or sabotage.

Monitor for data poisoning attacks that could corrupt training data.

19.7 Building Trust with Stakeholders

For successful adoption:

Regulators: Share model validation data and explain how AI respects safety standards.

Employees: Communicate that AI is a tool to enhance, not replace, human expertise.

Customers and the public: Publish sustainability and safety impact reports from AI projects.

19.8 Continuous Compliance Monitoring

Ethics and compliance are not one-time tasks:

Review AI models annually for alignment with new laws.

Conduct independent safety audits.

Maintain logs of AI recommendations and operator actions for traceability.

Chapter 20 – AI in Chemical Project Department

20.1 Introduction

The chemical industry operates at the intersection of high capital intensity, technological complexity, and stringent environmental and safety requirements. Every project, whether a greenfield plant, an expansion, or modernization of an existing unit, represents a massive orchestration of resources, knowledge, and regulatory compliance. The Project Department serves as the strategic hub that translates corporate objectives into operational reality, coordinating engineering disciplines, procurement, construction, commissioning, and eventual handover to operations.

Historically, chemical project departments relied on manual planning, spreadsheets, experience-based judgments, and conventional project management software. While this approach delivered many successful projects, it faced multiple challenges:

Cost Overruns: Fluctuating raw material prices, unplanned labor expenses, and unforeseen design changes often escalate budgets.

Schedule Delays: Construction timelines are disrupted by weather, vendor delays, permit issues, and engineering modifications.

Data Fragmentation: Disconnected departments and siloed information hinder coordination and timely decision-making.

Safety and Environmental Risk: Manual monitoring may fail to detect hazards proactively.

Knowledge Attrition: Experienced personnel retiring or changing roles lead to loss of institutional knowledge.

The emergence of Artificial Intelligence (AI) provides transformative solutions to these challenges. AI leverages large datasets—historical project records, real-time sensor data, vendor performance, financial and operational data—to generate predictive insights, optimize schedules, enhance procurement, and strengthen safety and environmental compliance. Beyond merely augmenting human decision-making, AI enables automation, predictive analytics, and digital simulations that fundamentally improve project outcomes.

AI is now a strategic necessity for chemical companies. From conceptualization to commissioning, AI empowers project teams to:

- Predict costs and timelines with higher accuracy
- Manage change and Version control of the documentation
- Optimize plant designs and resource allocation
- Automate repetitive tasks and minimize human error
- Enhance safety, environmental compliance, and sustainability
- Retain knowledge and improve decision-making across projects

The following sections will explore the full project life cycle, detailing how AI integrates at each stage, the benefits it delivers, challenges encountered, case studies of real implementations, comparison tables, and the skills required for future chemical project engineers.

20.2 Project Life Cycle in the Chemical Industry

A chemical project progresses through multiple stages, each with specific objectives, deliverables, and stakeholders. Understanding this life cycle is critical to implementing AI effectively.

20.2.1 Project Identification and Feasibility Studies

Project identification begins with the analysis of market opportunities, raw material availability, technology options, and strategic alignment. Feasibility studies evaluate technical, financial, and environmental viability.

Traditional method of project conceiving

- Select a range of chemicals, which may be, either existing product or totally new chemical to the company
- Upstream or raw material for any product. This is done to reduce cost of raw material
- Down streams product, which can utilize one of company product. This is done to increase the demand of existing product.
- Once these range of chemicals are selected.

Carry out Market survey for each product

Those promising chemicals having sufficient demand gap, including upcoming capacity, carry out prefeasibility or feasibility study.

Those promising among above having higher IRR and Payback, NPV than accepted, carryout detailed feasibility Report or DFR to confirm the financial attractiveness along with considering, sensitivity analysis, Sources of Technology availability, identifying source for raw materials and marketing regions and or big buyers.

Based on outcome of DFR and Fund availability with company, take decision to implement the same. The entire cycle of activity may take 12 months to 18 months to come to conclusion for implementation.

Project Profitability Matrix

	Item	Life of Project	IRR/ over BANK PLR	Payback
1	Green Field Project. New Product	20	11.4%/ 4%	7 Year
2	Green Field Project, Existing Product	15	12%/5%	6 Year
3	Brownfield Project, New Product	20	12%/5%	6 Year
4	Brownfield project, Existing Product	15	14%/7%	5 Year

Reasons of above is as follows

- New Product is having higher risk due to unknown zone.
- Greenfield Project require more infrastructure to be built.
- New Product under Brownfield use land at existing unit which is also a competitive opportunity cost not accounted for.
- Existing product in Brownfield project uses existing facilities as common infrastructure and having known uncertainty and hence having less risk.

Role of AI in project conceiving.

AI can reduce the cycle of activity using LLM like CHATGPT in few minutes to few hours and in fact, you can have 10 feasibility reports in few days and you can take decision for final product proposed to be implemented for the company and then carry out market survey and detailed feasibility report as a confirmatory market survey and DFR to take your final decision to implement the project.

Entire cycle with AI assisted can be reduced to 3 to six months to come to conclusion for implementation, which is more than 50% reduction in cycle time.

AI Integration:

Predictive Analytics: Machine learning models process historical market, production, and pricing data to forecast product demand and price trends.

Scenario Simulation: AI simulates multiple project scenarios, optimizing financial, operational, and environmental outcomes.

NLP for Regulatory Compliance: AI scans regulatory documents to identify constraints, compliance requirements, and potential risks.

Probabilistic Financial Modeling: AI evaluates outcomes across a range of input uncertainties, providing confidence intervals for investment decisions.

20.2.2 Project Execution.

Traditional method for project execution is as follows

1. Approval of Project
2. Tie up with Technology Supplier
3. Appointment Basic Engineering
4. Appointment of Detailed Engineering consultant
5. Procurement of Equipment and erection materials and accessories
6. Appointment Engineering all erection Services
7. Civil Engineering erection Services
8. Mechanical engineering erection Services
9. Electrical Engineering erection Service
10. Instrumentation Engineering erection Services
11. Approintment DCS Suppliers
12. Manpower suppliers

    or
13. Appointment of Turnkey erection Service for services for combination from 2 to 10.
14. Progress reporting or PMC consultant

There could be several other combination single vendors to increase reliability and responsibility of project progress to multiple vendors to reduce cost and have more controls.

Out of them only three options pro and cons are given below

A. LSTK Contract (Option)

Pro : Risk in price escalation is low

High cost due to high risk for contractor
Cons: Lower margin in design capacity and efficiency.
Low equipment design margin
Lower quality MOC in design

It needed that Contract/Agreement should be much more in detailed clauses about technical conditions else contractor may compromise quality.

B. Basic engineering + LSTK Erection (Option)

Pro : Price escalation risk is low

Cons: Better Equipment specification
Better Design margin can be fixed
Better Equipment/Pipe line margin to have easy Expandability.
Low coordination requirement among various erection contractor.
Higher Cost, however lower than single LSTK route due to lower financial risk for erection contractor

C. Basic Engineering + separate Erection Contractor (Civil, Mechanical, Electrical, Instrument) (Option)
Pro: Lower Price
Higher risk of price and time escalation
Cons: Design margin at owner control
Equipment/Pipeline Margin at owner control.
High coordination requirement among all contractor for any change in design.
Better control over Vendor selection of critical equipment for maintaining high quality.

Role of AI in project Engineering can be

Document Management/Change Management,

Version control: during Project execution, changes in document management take place during course of action of Basic Engineering and Detailed Engineering and Procurement. This due to discussions that take place between Technology supplier, Basic Engineering group, Detail Engineering group and Vendors.

AI can keep tab of latest version of Documents distributed to relevant persons.

AI can ensure that changes done in one document should reflect in all relevant documents and redistribute it to all relevant personnels

AI can ensure that modification in documents, which are already released for procurement enquiry and redistribute to relevant personnels and bidders.

AI can ensure changes in specification of one equipment reflect to other equipment specifications and redistribute to relevant personnel and bidders.

AI can ensure that only latest specification is getting released for enquiry and reissue of modification in enquiry if required

AI can maintain document labeling "Good for Tendering" or "Good for Construction".

AI can keep tab of progress of Basic or detail Engineering, procurement and erection and commissioning and issue alarms/critical alarm to relevant persons for delay affecting critical-path activity.

AI can keep tab on delay in approval of documents and issue alarm to relevant personnel.

AI can accurately predict erection material quantity so that contingency can be reduced and no of takeoff of various erection material can be reduced.

AI can procure items faster and cheaper material.

AI also ensure less wastage consequently less cost.

AI Accurately predict delivery schedule with tolerance available for time and issue alarms to project personnel for any change in delivery and give early alarm for delays.

If any critical deliveries is getting missed, suggest appropriate action to be undertaken to reduce/nullify its effect on overall project schedule to project manager of owner and other personnels.

Ensure that adequate front is available for the contractor to work during construction phase.

If project is getting delayed then then give you different alternative method for reducing the delays

Procurement of Equipment and erection materials and accessories

Traditional method to carry out procurement are as follows

1. Finalization of acceptable Vendor List after owner approval.
2. Release of Technical specification of Equipment and bill of materials for long delivery items,
3. Release of Technical and Commercial terms of conditions
4. Send it owner for its concurrence
5. Preparing Tender documents and releasing enquiries to prequalified bidders or through other means, either in two stage or three stage bidding
6. For three stage bidding, Finalize Prequalification criteria with concurrence of Owner.
7. Receive offer from bidders and distribute it for comments.
8. For two stage bidders, release technical queries(TQs) on the offer. Received TQs answered and release TQ2 and so on till all TQs are answered
9. Prepare a comparative table for all the technical offer and obtain approval of Technically acceptable offers recommend rejection of not acceptable offers.
10. Define any loading criteria among technically qualified bidders.
11. Obtain approval for the above step 9 and 10
12. Release Commercial queries(CQ) receive the answer of CQ till al CQs are offered.
13. Prepare a comparative table of commercial offers including loading criteria for all qualified parties.
14. Obtain approval for placement of order on most preferred bidder.
15. Issue Letter of Intent

16. Issue detailed purchase Order based on offer, TQs and CQs.
17. Follow same procedure for not so long delivery items.
18. Carry out stage wise or final inspection
19. Release of payment for procured material either after delivery or stage wise as agreed in purchase offer.

Procurement of erection materials based on latest layout and P& I Diagrams/Engineering flow Diagram.

- Estimate of quantities of Erection material, for long delivery time and availability of specification.
- Based on estimate decide the bifurcation of enquiry for same category item and release Takeoff one for enquiries
- Wait for enough detail for Takeoff two material and release for enquiries.
- Follow above procurement procedures for all general erection materials.

AI Can assist project team in following way.

- AI can have very significant roles in following activities.
- AI can help in Finalizing Vendors list
- AI can finalize prequalification criteria ensuring enough competition in procurement.
- AI can help in Preparing Technical specification
- AI can help in finalizing Commercial terms and conditions.
- AI can help Tender Document and release it to vendors or press.
- AI can Prepare initial technical comparative table of offer and finalize Technical Queries to be asked from each bidder.
- AI can Prepare, based on answer of technical queries by bidder, a Final technical comparative table.
- AI can help in preparing loading criteria for any acceptable technical deviations.
- AI can prepare initial commercial comparative table ask Commercial queries from each bidder and then prepare final comparative table based on the answer given by bidders.

- Ai can suggest loading criteria for acceptable commercial condition deviations.
- AI can help in finalizing final approval notes for management
- AI can help in preparing LOI and Purchase order.
- AI can assist in preparing Bill of Quantities erection materials and help in procurement of them.
- AI also can split order, for reducing risk for the best advantage to owner.
- Apart from above AI can help finalizing the treatment of non-quoted items for erection material. In place of rejecting entire offer AI can suggest better ways by splitting offer to the best advantage of owner.
- AI can help in releasing payment for procured material as PO terms
- AI can schedule the release of enquiries, release LOI and release of purchase order and inspection visit so that optimum utilization of available manpower can take place. This will shorten project procurement schedule.

Progress Reporting

Traditional method of continuous project progress reporting was

Project manager was getting reports from individual head and combining all report and then make a consolidated report for forwarding it to project director or Owner.

AI can automate it using visual photographs either at fixed camera takes photograph at certain frequency or use of drone video and photograph of entire site at certain frequency.

AI tool can be used to detect mile stone completion and send automatic/semiautomatic progress report preparation to some extent.

20.2.3 Further bifurcation of Project stages can be done as follows

1 Conceptual and Basic Engineering

Conceptual and basic engineering translates feasibility into initial design, including process, equipment, and preliminary layout decisions.

Key Activities of Basic Engineering:

- Block Flow Diagrams (BFDs): Outline major process streams, material inputs/outputs, and preliminary sizing.
- Preliminary Equipment Sizing: Estimate capacities, energy requirements, and utility needs.
- Site Selection: Evaluate geography, accessibility, transportation need for raw material and product along with location of customer location and regulatory constraints.
- Lay out finalization based on available site size and orientation
- Preliminary Cost Estimates: Develop approximate CAPEX and OPEX for decision-making.

AI Integration:

Process Optimization: AI-driven simulation tools optimize process parameters, throughput, and energy efficiency.

Generative Layout Design: AI generates multiple plant layouts and ranks them based on cost, safety, and energy performance.

Site Selection algorithms: AI integrates geographic, environmental, and regulatory data and transportation requirement of raw material and product based on customer location, to suggest optimal plant locations.

Cost Estimation: Machine learning models trained on historical projects provide more accurate preliminary estimates.

2 Detailed Engineering

Detailed engineering creates construction-ready specifications and designs.

Key Activities:

- Piping and Instrumentation Diagrams (P&IDs): Detailed design of all process piping and instrumentation.
- Civil, Mechanical, Electrical, and Instrumentation drawings: precise specifications for construction.
- Equipment Selection: finalize vendors, materials, and technical specifications.
- Integration with Licensors: Ensure technology compliance and design fidelity.

AI Integration:

Automated CAD Tools: AI generates layouts and drawings while detecting design clashes.

Knowledge Capture: AI repositories store lessons learned from prior projects for reference.

Error Detection: AI identifies inconsistencies or violations of design standards.

3. Procurement

Procurement secures equipment, materials, and services necessary for construction.

Challenges in Traditional Procurement:

- Manual vendor evaluation leads to suboptimal selection.
- Contract reviews are time-consuming.
- Supply chain disruptions can delay projects.

AI Integration:

Vendor Analysis: AI ranks suppliers using quality, delivery, and cost metrics.

AI can automate procurement Activities like

- Preparation of Technical and Commercial part of enquiries
- Issue of Tender Documents to Vendor list already finalized

- Evaluation of technical offer through TQs and their answer given by Vendors.
- Prepare comparative table of technical offers received.
- Recommendation proposal for accepting technical acceptable offer.
- Prepare comparative Table of commercial offers for Technical qualified offers.
- Recommendation proposal for selection of Vendor.
- Issue of LOI and Detailed Purchase offer.

Contract Analytics: NLP scans contracts to highlight risks or non-compliance clauses.

Predictive Supply Chain: AI predicts delays and suggests contingency plans.

Procurement Optimization: AI schedules deliveries and allocates resources efficiently to minimize idle time.

4 Construction and Commissioning

The construction phase executes the design on-site, followed by commissioning to ensure operational readiness.

Challenges:

- Coordination of thousands of interdependent tasks.
- Maintaining safety in hazardous environments.
- Monitoring quality and progress manually.

AI Integration:

Dynamic Scheduling: Reinforcement learning adjusts schedules in real time.

Safety Monitoring: Computer vision detects unsafe actions and PPE violations.

Progress Tracking: Drones capture site images, compared with 3D models to assess completion.

Predictive Commissioning: AI predicts equipment failures, reducing start-up risks.

5. Operation and Handover

The final phase transitions the project to operations.

Activities:

- Operator training using manuals, simulations, and digital twins.
- Project closure reporting and documentation.
- Post-project performance assessment and lessons learned.

AI Integration:

- Digital twins provide interactive training.
- AI retrieves commissioning and operational data for reference.
- Performance analytics optimize initial operations.

Chapter 21 - Artificial Intelligence in Chemical Project Construction

Introduction

Chemical project construction is one of the most critical stages in the lifecycle of a chemical project. It involves translating detailed engineering designs into physical infrastructure. That is why a separate chapter is provided. This phase includes civil works, structural erection, mechanical equipment installation, piping, electrical systems, instrumentation, automation, and safety systems. Traditionally, chemical project construction has faced recurring challenges such as cost overruns, delays, safety incidents, and poor coordination among several sub departments

Artificial Intelligence (AI) is emerging as a transformative force in construction management. By leveraging big data, machine learning, computer vision, and predictive analytics, AI is improving efficiency, enhancing safety, and enabling better decision-making in chemical project construction. This chapter explores the role of AI in construction management, practical applications, case studies, challenges, and future perspectives.

21.1 Overview of Chemical Project Construction

The construction phase of a chemical project typically includes:

- **Site Preparation:** Clearing, leveling, and preparing land.
- **Civil Works:** Foundations, roads, drainage, and structures.
- **Mechanical Installation:** Equipment erection, piping, and other structures.

- **Electrical:** Installation of cables, MCCs, Motors, Transformer and other Electrical systems.
- **Instrumentation:** Installation of cables, Sensors, Transmitters, DCS, PLCs, and control systems. Automation and Safety Systems: Deployment of advanced control systems and safety interlocks.
- **Pre-commissioning Activities**: Testing, inspection, flushing, and calibration.

This phase is resource-intensive and requires precise coordination among contractors, suppliers, and project teams.

21.2 Challenges in Traditional Chemical Project Construction

- **Cost Overruns:** Unanticipated material price hikes, poor planning, or scope changes.
- **Delays:** Weather disruptions, supply chain bottlenecks, labor shortages, and poor scheduling.
- **Change Management:** Changes carryout in design stage sometime get missed in specifications revision and ultimately result in last minutes modification only after noticing the mistakes very late, during erection and it leads to compromise in quality of equipment,
- **Safety Risks:** Construction sites pose hazards such as falls, fires, chemical exposure, and equipment accidents.
- **Coordination Issues:** Multiple contractors and subcontractors increase complexity.
- **Quality Assurance:** Welder Qualification, Defects in welding, material handling, or installation cause rework and delays.
- **Regulatory Compliance:** Meeting stringent safety, environmental, and labor standards.

AI provides new tools to tackle these issues effectively.

21.3 AI Applications in Chemical Project Construction

AI in Project Scheduling and Planning

- AI algorithms analyze historical data to predict construction timelines more accurately.
- Dynamic scheduling tools adapt automatically to delays (e.g., weather or supply issues).
- AI assists in resource leveling by optimizing allocation of labor, equipment, and materials.

AI in Site Monitoring

- **Computer Vision:** Drones and cameras feed data into AI models that track construction progress in real time.
- **Safety Compliance:** AI detects violations such as missing PPE or unsafe work practices.
- **Material Tracking:** AI-powered systems monitor material movement and stock levels.

AI in Equipment and Workforce Management

- Predictive analytics forecast equipment downtime, enabling preventive maintenance.
- AI platforms match labor availability with project needs, optimizing workforce deployment.
- Autonomous vehicles and robots handle repetitive construction tasks.

AI in Quality Assurance

- AI detects welding defects, cracks, or corrosion using image recognition.
- Predictive models forecast potential failure points, reducing rework.

- NLP-based systems automatically analyze inspection reports for trends and anomalies.

AI in Supply Chain and Procurement

- AI predicts demand and optimizes procurement schedules.
- Machine learning models forecast price fluctuations for critical materials (e.g., steel, cement).
- AI improves logistics by predicting delivery times and preventing stockouts.

AI in Health, Safety, and Environment (HSE)

- AI-driven wearables monitor worker fatigue, heart rate, and exposure to harmful gases.
- Predictive models identify high-risk areas for accidents.
- Computer vision monitors compliance with environmental regulations (e.g., waste disposal, emissions).

21.4 Digital Twins in Construction

Digital twins integrate AI, IoT, and BIM (Building Information Modeling) to create virtual replicas of construction sites. Applications include:

- Real-time monitoring of progress.
- Virtual simulations of construction sequences to identify bottlenecks.
- Clash detection in 3D models before physical execution.
- Enhanced collaboration between project stakeholders.

21.5 Case Studies of AI in Chemical Project Construction

Case Study 1: Refinery Expansion

AI-powered scheduling reduced project delays by 20%. Drone-based AI monitoring improved progress reporting and safety compliance.

Case Study 2: Fertilizer Plant Greenfield Project

AI-assisted digital twins helped in clash detection during piping and structural installation, saving millions in rework costs.

Case Study 3: AI for Worker Safety

Wearable AI devices deployed in a petrochemical plant construction site reduced accident rates by 30% by detecting fatigue and issuing early warnings.

21.6 Benefits of AI in Chemical Project Construction

- More accurate project schedules and budgets.
- Improved worker safety and reduced incidents.
- Better quality assurance with reduced rework.
- Enhanced efficiency in material and workforce management.
- Greater transparency through real-time monitoring and reporting.

21.7 Challenges in Adopting AI for Construction

- High Capital Costs: AI-enabled systems, drones, and wearables require significant investment.
- Data Quality Issues: Inconsistent or incomplete data hampers AI accuracy.
- Integration Barriers: Linking AI tools with existing ERP, BIM, and project management systems is challenging.
- Workforce Resistance: Construction teams may resist digital transformation due to lack of training.
- Cybersecurity Concerns: Increased connectivity creates risks of cyberattacks.

21.8 Future of AI in Chemical Project Construction

- Autonomous Construction Sites: Use of AI-guided robots for welding, lifting, and installation.

- AI-Integrated BIM Platforms: Seamless integration of design, scheduling, and execution in real time.
- Sustainability-Driven AI Tools: Optimizing resource use, waste reduction, and carbon footprint.
- Collaborative AI Ecosystems: Cloud-based AI platforms enabling multiple stakeholders to collaborate effectively.

21.9 Skills Required for Future Construction Engineers

- Proficiency in AI-powered project management software.
- Knowledge of digital twins, drones, and computer vision applications.
- Data analytics and machine learning fundamentals.
- Strong understanding of HSE compliance with AI integration.
- Cross-disciplinary collaboration skills.

Part Four

Integration Strategy & Future

Chapter 22 – Case Studies from the Chemical Industry

Artificial Intelligence is no longer confined to pilot projects or academic studies in the chemical sector — it is delivering measurable business results.

This chapter presents selected real-world examples that demonstrate AI's impact on R&D, manufacturing, maintenance, and the supply chain.

22.1 Chemical Giant A– Accelerating Materials Discovery

Challenge:

Developing new polymers and coatings often involves years of lab trials, costing millions in R&D.

AI Application: they implemented machine learning algorithms to analyze historical experimental data and simulate the properties of new materials before physical synthesis.

Outcome:

Reduced material development cycles by up to 50%.

Increased probability of successful formulation in early testing.

Key Takeaway: AI can turn the "trial-and-error" process into "trial-and-compute," saving both time and cost.

22.2 Chemical Giant B– Predictive Maintenance at Scale

Challenge:

They operates thousands of pumps, compressors, and heat exchangers across plants worldwide. Unexpected failures could cost millions in downtime and safety incidents.

AI Application: They deployed predictive maintenance models using vibration, temperature, and pressure sensor data, combined with historical failure records.

Outcome:

Reduced unplanned downtime by 20–25%.

Extended equipment life and reduced spare parts inventory.

Key Takeaway: Predictive maintenance allows better planning and resource allocation, directly improving plant reliability.

22.3 Chemical Giant C – AI-Driven Supply Chain Optimization

Challenge:

With a global customer base and volatile feedstock markets, they needed to better match production with demand.

AI Application: Implemented demand forecasting and dynamic scheduling algorithms that integrate market data, weather trends, and customer orders.

Outcome:

Improved forecast accuracy by 15–20%.

Reduced logistics costs by 8% through optimized routing.

Key Takeaway: In chemicals, accurate forecasting is not just about avoiding shortages — it's about avoiding costly overproduction.

22.4 Chemical Giant D – Real-Time Process Optimization

Challenge:

Complex batch processes required constant operator intervention to maintain product quality.

AI Application: Deployed real-time optimization models that adjusted process parameters automatically, based on inline sensor readings and predictive analytics.

Outcome:

Reduced off-spec batches by 30%.

Lowered energy consumption per batch by 12%.

Key Takeaway: AI can continuously fine-tune operations in a way that manual adjustments cannot match.

22.5 Chemical Giant E – Enhancing Safety with AI Vision Systems

Challenge:

Ensuring compliance with PPE (personal protective equipment) rules across large industrial sites is challenging.

AI Application: Installed computer vision systems connected to site CCTV to detect PPE violations in real-time and alert supervisors.

Outcome:

Increased PPE compliance to above 95%.

Reduced safety incident rates significantly.

Key Takeaway: AI can strengthen safety culture without slowing operations.

22.6 Lessons Learned Across Case Studies

From these examples, several success factors emerge:

Data Quality First: Poor or inconsistent data undermines even the best algorithms.

Human-AI Collaboration: AI works best when domain experts remain in the loop.

Scalable Platforms: Start small, but ensure technology can expand plant-wide or globally.

Clear ROI Targets: Successful projects have measurable business goals from the start.

Chapter 23 – Building the AI Roadmap for a Chemical Company

Artificial Intelligence offers transformative potential for the chemical industry — but without a structured adoption plan, many AI projects fail to move beyond pilots. A well-crafted AI roadmap ensures investments are targeted, risks are managed, and benefits are sustained.

23.1 Define the AI Vision and Strategic Objectives

Every AI journey begins with a clear vision aligned to corporate strategy:

Profitability: Improve yields, reduce downtime, and optimize the supply chain.

Sustainability: Reduce carbon footprint through process optimization.

Safety: Minimize human exposure to hazardous processes.

Tip: Avoid vague objectives like "use AI in our plants" — instead, use measurable targets such as "reduce energy specific consumption per ton by 5% in 18 months."

23.2 Cross-Functional AI Team Center of Excellence

AI in chemicals requires expertise from multiple domains:

Chemical engineers: Provide process insights and constraints.

Data scientists: Build and tune AI models.

IT/OT teams: Handle data integration, cybersecurity, and plant connectivity.

Operations leaders: Ensure solutions are practical and scalable.

Structure: Create an AI Center of Excellence (CoE) that supports all plants.

Recruitment for team member of Center of Excellence should be from one to two numbers from Data Science knowledge, one to two members` machine learning, One to two members from Agentic AI or prompt engineering, one Chemical Engineers, Two Instrument Engineer, Two IT Engineer, one Mechanical & one Electrical Maintenance Engineers. Include champions of all department to support core of excellence.

Provide exposure of, AI concepts for all Center of Excellence team member including Champion members representing the core departments.

Center of Excellence and Champions should decide path to implement AI in few departments the company.

Job of Center of Excellence shall also be that prioritize the path of implementation. They will also select which AI tool should be used for the required function. How AI agent should be developed for which purpose. Taking help from outside for which AI implementation.

There also should also be team formed for the department it needs to be implemented containing at two additional members from core department apart from members from Center of excellence.

23.3 Audit and Prepare Data Assets

AI success depends on data quality and availability. Key steps:

Inventory existing data from DCS, PLC, MES, LIMS, ERP, and supply chain systems.

Assess gaps: Missing sensor data, unstructured lab notes, or poor historical records.

Clean and integrate: Standardize data formats, remove noise, and align timestamps.

Note: Data governance — defining ownership, privacy, and security — should be set from day one.

23.4 Prioritize High-Impact Use Cases

Not all AI projects are worth pursuing immediately. Select use cases based on:

Business value (cost savings, revenue growth, risk reduction).

Feasibility (data readiness, technical complexity, regulatory constraints).

Time to value (quick wins build momentum).

Example high-impact areas:

1. Procurement automation,
2. predictive maintenance,
3. demand forecasting.
4. energy optimization,
5. quality prediction,

Low hanging fruits should be first implemented few of the low hanging fruit is

1. Procurement automation
2. Predictive maintenance
3. Progress reporting
4. Demand forecasting.
5. Cash flow prediction
6. Faster recruitment

Implementation guide for procurement automation/Maintenance Department/Marketing Department/Finance Department/HR department is described as follows. But instruction AI implementation in any department.

23.5 Start with Pilots, Then Scale

Pilot phase:

Test the AI model on a small process unit or product line.

Measure key metrics: accuracy, downtime reduction, yield improvement.

Scaling phase:

Deploy across multiple plants or business units.

Automate retraining of models with new data.

Best practice: Document lessons learned from each pilot before scaling.

23.6 Procurement Automation

Procurement action starts from requirement generation to delivery of item at site again to consumption of item in plant/project. There is several of obstacles for completing procurement. Major steps in procurement are as follows.

1. Finalizing item specification, special technical conditions and estimate required quantity.
2. Taking approval for floating Tender, finalize vendor list, special terms and condition and general terms and Condition.
3. Float Tender to approved vendor list or float on open tender through Newspaper advertisement or float Website based floating of Tender.
4. Receive bids on due date, Open bids and send it to user for technical evaluation.
5. Receive Technical queries(TQ) from user and parallelly make Commercial queries(CQ), send it to bidders. Receive answer of TQ and CQ. Follow this cycle till all TQ and CQ are answer by all bidders.
6. Make Technical and Commercial comparative statement.
7. Take approval for rejecting any offer and any loading criteria for acceptable deviation in technical and commercial conditions.

8. Open commercial bids of technical acceptable bidders, make commercial comparative statement. Make bid evaluation for lowest cost to owner including loading criteria.
9. Obtain approval for final acceptance offer of most preferred bidder.
10. Place LOI and Purchase order to successful bidder.

For medium size tender for activity 1 to 3 take 4 to 8 weeks for floating tender we may give 2 to 3 week time for bid submission by bidders. For activity 4 to 9 may take 8 to 12 weeks. This makes total time 14 to 23 weeks in normal course. This is repetitive task and procurement officer continue to remain busy in repetitive task. AI will make them free for more productive jobs.

AI can very easily handle this repetitive task and reduce the cycle time.

One AI agent can do the task of preparation of Tender documents.

AI tools can float tender after taking approval using SAP API.

AI tool can mask vendor details from offer before evaluation.

2nd AI agent can assist in technical evaluation by preparing initial and final comparative statement of technical offer and suggest TQs to be asked to bidders.

3rd AI agent can assist in Commercial evaluation by preparing initial and final comparative statement of commercial offer and suggest CQs to be asked by bidders.

4rth AI agent can assist in preparing approval note for rejecting offer and loading criteria for technical/commercial deviations.

5th AI agent can assist in preparing approval note for final acceptance of offer of most preferred bidders.

2nd AI tool will prepare and issue LOI and Purchase order based on TQs and CQs of successful bidder using SAP API.

These AI agents will do all repetitive task of procurement officer and reduce their load and he can concentrate only in overseeing task and strategies finalization.

The considerable reduction in total cycle time can be achieved using AI.

After placement of purchase order AI can track progress of delivery, any delays and also track risk of delivery failure and alert can be generated to relevant persons for taking appropriate actions.

After delivery final inspection for acceptance of material and release of payment can normally take 30 days. This cycle time can also be reduced if desired. AI will track final inspection for acceptance after which material can be stock charge and used

Apart from this AI can be implemented to help in procurement department in accurately predicting the consumption of general item by Machine Learning and advance algorithm. So that placement of yearly order and delivery will be faster or in-fact it can be on demand supply within already agreed few days.

Consumption of General items is to be predicted first using neural network and finally regressing and arriving at algorithm to predict accurate consumption.

23.7 AI implementation in Maintenance Department

Maintenance department can be benefited by implementation of AI from following improved situation

A. Unscheduled breakdown
B. Spare parts consumption
C. Improved inspection

To implement AI in maintenance department first an AI build a team with knowledge of machine learning and Data Science including core maintenance engineer. Then we have to ensure that availability of data is sufficient to doing regression and Machine learning. Then only further implementation can be carried forward. The AI team will decide the pathway to implementation based on data availability and financial benefit. Here we are discussing about mechanical maintenance but it can also be related electrical or instrument maintenance cases. Team has to identify improvement of which case is more important.

A. Unscheduled breakdown

If maintenance is facing unscheduled breakdown in machineries. First step is to choose few machineries with high failure rate and for which sufficient data is available.

Initially use neural network to find important parameters and critical component which affect the failure. Then regress the failure data and component failure data using machine learning, to predict failure of component's life. Once team is able to predict the component life. Improve the accuracy of prediction up to an acceptable level by modifying the algorithm by including new parameters.

Once, high accuracy level in prediction is reached, start issuing alert of failure with balance life till next failure of critical components, to relevant team members for taking necessary maintenance job at next available opportunity. This reporting will reduce the failure rate due to accurate prediction of component life. After AI prediction is acceptable in one machine implement 2nd machine either in similar nature or choose different kind of machines for gaining more confidence. After this stage is successful, solution can be implemented similar machines throughout company.

B. Spare Part Consumption

Let AI team to identify few (may be top five) high consumption items. Take initial help of neural network a learning tool to find about interaction of various parameters like life, seasons, load of machinery/plant, MOC of item, corrosivity, density, viscosity of fluid handled by machinery with consumption. Select parameter having high correlation with consumption. Then start regressing consumption with the selected parameter by data scientist.

In next stage start predicting the consumption of all items. Monitor accuracy of prediction. Improve the prediction by adding new parameters other than initially selected, till high accuracy of all of the above items is achieved. Start predicting consumption on weekly or monthly basis.

In next stage, start generating requirement to procurement team with manual override considering present stock, delivery time and procurement time. This will be done using SAP API.

Once enough confidence is developed, reduce manual intervention and implement it on other spare parts procurements.

C. Improved Inspection

Apart from normal inspection carried out by maintenance department an automated inspection can be carried out with help of AI with the help photos/video or audio recording.

For example a moving vehicle can record audio sounds and AI tool can be trained to identify any defect in either yard piping or in a location which is not possible to have frequent inspection by human being, for making observation due to higher risk or any other reasons. Audio sound can be related to steam trap failure in yard or it can related to either the any gas or superheated steam leakage, this leakage which can not identified by only naked eye. Relate location of vehicle at the time sound recording to identify the leaking trap identification or leakage point. These inspections can be done at regular frequency say on for trap failure weekly basis and for gas/steam leakages on daily basis, for faster detection of trap failure or Steam/Gas leakages to minimize the loss of steam and gas by early maintenance.

Similarly photograph at regular interval or a video can be used for identifying liquid leakage or solid spillages or overflow of bin or transfer tower for early remedial action. Even video can be used to detect off-center of conveyor belts in long isolated unmanned gantry, this will detect event in early stage, system may generate alarm to relevant team, to minimize the spillage of material by taking early corrective measures.

23.8 AI Imlementation in project department

Make team for AI implementation in project should consist of one mechanical, electrical, Instrument engineer apart from two to three member from Center of excellence. Team shall be identifying the area in which AI implementation should be done first.

Project Department have two sections One section which only plan the upcoming project 2nd section consist execution of approved project.

Low hanging fruit in project planning section of project department are

a) Market Survey
b) Project Cost Estimation.

A. **Market Survey**

Large Language Model(LLM) can be used generating market survey report. A LLM with proper prompts can predict demand within country. Supply position in the country and any import or export which is exist to fill up the unfulfilled demand gap or having export potential.

B. **Project Cost Estimation**

LLM can also predict project cost using proper prompt, considering fluctuation in prices of metals. AI can also predict working capital requirement. AI can also be used to develop dedicated software using no coding techniques, for estimating equipment cost.

We can also have AI assisted tendering for arriving at budgetary cost of equipment and to check accuracy of above developed software.

Once Project cost estimation is accurate, feasibility report shall also be realistic.

Low hanging fruit for Project Execution section shall be

a) Documents control
b) Procurement

c) Progress reporting
d) Tracking Delays
e) Manpower deployment

A. Document Control

AI tool can be deployed for tracking all document and its versions. After every revision in documents, AI will ensure that revised document has been redistributed to all relevant personnel.

Another AI tool can be deployed to identify and do corrections in various other document/ specification/ parameters which uses these changed data.

B. Procurement

Detailed Automation in procurement department is already given in earlier portion of chapter, hence it is not repeated here again, same measures can be adopted here also.

AI tool can used for predicted quantity of general items so that it's procurement can be preempted based on availability of information from engineering activity.

AI can also phase the procurement scheduling based on upcoming procurement activities.

AI can also deploy additional manpower for reducing procurement phase of project.

C. Progress reporting

AI tool can be deployed for collecting data for progress reporting from various sources.

Another AI Agent can be deployed for preparing standard progress report suitable for following phases of project.

- Engineering
- Procurement
- Delivery at site.
- Site preparation

- Erection
- Commissioning

Hence a standard report can be generated at click of button for each phase of project and over all progress report.

D. Tracking Delays

Any project's success depends on timely completion. Very peculiar situation for project delay is that even one item delay if remain unchecked can delay entire project. Hence delay of every single item is very critical for entire project success.

AI tool can track delays based on current phase of project.

Engineering Phase

AI tool can track release of documents from Engineering department and will also track comment/approval from relevant department.

AI can also track no of document released vs no of document scheduled to be released as per original master schedule and hence can track % completion.

Separate AI tool can track no of document for which comment/approval is pending after elapse of fixed days after release say 15 days.

AI can issue alert to relevant persons for taking corrective actions.

Procurement

AI tool can track delay in release of enquiries after fixed days from release of specification and quantities from Engineering department.

Another AI tool can track delay in evaluation of technical/commercial offer or delay in Vendor response after scheduled period allotted to them

3rd AI tool can track delay in LOI/PO placement after fixed days of evaluation completed.

4rth tool can track delay in inspection call/inspection completion.

5th AI tool can track delay in delivery or delivery risk of item.

6th AI tool can track delay in construction

7th AI tool can track over all delay in project schedule.

8rth AI tool can track delay in commissioning and stabilization.

9th tool can track affect on project profitability due to delay in delivery or change in cost of items, in real time.

E. Manpower deployment

AI tool can be deployed to track delay in project schedule due to shortage of manpower in every discipline. AI can suggest predict additional manpower deployment to reduce/eliminate delays.

AI can also do predictive hiring to avoid manpower shortage during project execution.

23.9 AI Implementation in Chemical Marketing Department

For implementing AI in Marketing department make a AI team with specialist from Central of Excellence member having specialization of data analytic, AI modelling and machine learning and at least two members of core group from the marketing department, out of two one could be already identified. This team will be marketing department specific. Their first job is to identify the area where AI can be implemented and identify low hanging fruits. Low hanging fruit of AI benefit in marketing department are

A. Demand forecasting.

B. Price Optimization

A. Demand forecasting

Data for sales for each product along with Prices, discount given to different grade of customers. These data along with market size growth, effect of seasons on demand, customer production plan is used to regress market demand. Initially use Neural network to be used finding parameter having high correlation coefficient with demand of product. Then finalize algorithm of demand prediction and parameters. Them improve the prediction with acceptable level of accuracy by including new parameter or changing algorithmic. Then use these demand predictions for advantage to the company in price optimization.

B. Price Optimization

Once demand prediction is accurate. Start estimating supply prediction using competitor's activity like production plan. Determine the unfulfilled demand or surplus of product availability. Use AI and these data for price fixation of product and volume discount. For this, use an algorithm to arrive at a price with maximum advantage to company.

Use AI, predicted demand data and shutdown planning data of all producing and all customer companies along with product cost arrived after considering raw material price fluctuation, competitive use of product, to predict best sale price of products for the company to give maximum contribution.

23.10 AI Implementation in Finance Department

For implementing AI in Finance departments make a AI team with specialist from Central of Excellence member having specialization of data analytic, AI modelling and machine learning and at least two members from the finance department, out of two one could be already identified champion of the department. This team will be department specific to finance. Their first job is to identify the area where AI can be implemented and low hanging fruits in Finance department. Low hanging fruit from Finance department are

a) Cash Flow prediction
b) Financial reporting

A. **Cash Flow prediction**

For Implementing AI for this job, develop a AI tool to calculate cash inflow in real time and future cash inflow prediction initially for 3 months. Once desired accuracy is achieved expand the time horizon of prediction to 6 months. This tool shall initially consider for following parameter

Real time cash inflow and predicted cash outflow.

- Predicted account receivable from sales already done and predicted sales of the product for which payment shall be received during the period of prediction.
- Payment collection time for sold products.
- Account payable for already placed PO,
- Amount to be paid for predicted PO to be placed for which payment shall be released during the period of prediction.

Another AI agent shall predict Future PO price of the items using AI developed software models for price of items also considering the fluctuation in price of raw materials of the product. This predicted price shall be considered for future PO value of the item for which PO shall be placed by the company.

- AI tool can track any anticipated delay in delivery predicted.
- Capital Investment forecast
- Other Payments like Wages and Salary, Bonus, Interest payment to Bank or other entity etc.

Improve prediction by comparing Actual vs predicted cash flow and analyze the difference using AI, try to reduce the difference considering more parameters.

B. **Financial Reporting.**

Identify which reports are to made by AI first, implementation phase. Develop software using AI for collecting data and generate contents without actually coding the software. Initially use these reports for feedback for improvements. Once accuracy for data collection reach

100% and satisfactory level of content generation. Then take 2nd batch of reports for generating them through AI.

23.11 AI Implementation in HR Department

For implementing AI in HR departments make a AI team with specialist from Central of Excellence member having specialization of data analytic, AI modelling and machine learning and at least two members from the HR department, out of two one could be already identified champion of the department. This team will be HR department specific. Their first job is to identify the area where AI can be implemented and low hanging fruits in HR department. Low hanging fruit from HR department are

a) Faster recruitment

b) Training

A. **Faster Recruitment**

HR department's best benefit of AI implementation is faster recruitment. For implementing AI in recruitment.

- AI agent can be deployed for collecting resume.
- Another AI agent can be developed for screening the collected resumes and ranking the resume for suitability for the company.
- This should be verified manually, for confirmation in initial phases be autonomous use
- Another AI agent can be used for scheduling interview call.
- AI tool can be used for preparing possible questionnaire for assisting Interviewer.

In the above process recruitment cycle time can be reduced at least by 30-40%.

AI can also be used for predicted hiring so that no shortage of manpower is experienced even after expansion takes place in the company.

B. **Training**

AI tool can be deployed for training need identification of all groups of employees.

For this Employee can be divided into several group. Then start using AI tool for training need identification of one or more group.

another AI tool can be used for preparing training calendar without affecting their normal work.

23.12 Integrate AI into Daily Operations

AI should not remain a “special project” — it must be embedded into standard workflows:

Operator dashboards: Show AI recommendations in real time.

Automated alerts: Push predictions to maintenance and quality teams.

Closed-loop control: In mature cases, let AI adjust process parameters autonomously (with human oversight).

23.13 Invest in Skills and Change Management

Even the best AI solution can fail if people resist using it.

Upskill plant staff on interpreting AI outputs.

Train managers on data-driven decision-making.

Communicate early about benefits and limits to build trust.

Tip: Position AI as a tool that augments human expertise, not replaces it.

23.14 Manage Risks and Compliance

The chemical industry faces strict safety and environmental regulations.

Ensure AI outputs are traceable and explainable.

Test models under edge-case conditions.

Build cybersecurity safeguards into connected systems.

23.15 Monitor, Evaluate, and Evolve

AI is not "set and forget."

Regularly review performance metrics.

Retrain models when process conditions change.

Experiment with emerging technologies like generative AI for R&D or AI-powered robotics.

Chapter 24 – Emerging AI Trends in the Chemical Industry

The chemical industry stands on the verge of a technology inflection point. While today's AI applications often focus on process optimization, predictive maintenance, and demand forecasting, tomorrow's AI will transform plant operations, R&D, and business models.

24.1 Autonomous Chemical Plants

Self-optimizing production: AI agents that continuously adjust parameters without human intervention.

Dynamic scheduling: AI balancing multiple production lines based on real-time market demand.

Integrated safety systems: AI detecting hazards and initiating automated emergency responses.

Current status: Early pilots in oil & gas and bulk chemicals; full autonomy is still years away but accelerating.

24.2 AI-Driven Sustainability

Carbon footprint minimization: AI optimizing processes to reduce greenhouse gas emissions.

Waste valorization: Turning by-products into valuable inputs using AI-guided chemical pathways.

Circular chemistry: AI models designing recyclable and biodegradable materials from the outset.

Regulatory pressure (net zero targets) is making sustainability a competitive advantage, not just a compliance requirement.

24.3 Generative AI for Materials Discovery

Inverse design: Starting from desired properties and using AI to propose novel molecular structures.

Multiscale modeling: Combining molecular dynamics, quantum chemistry, and process simulation in a unified AI framework.

Accelerated lab-to-market timelines: Months instead of years for new catalysts, polymers, or specialty chemicals.

24.4 AI + IoT + Robotics Integration

Smart sensors: Edge AI processing data directly at the measurement point, enabling instant response.

Autonomous inspection drones: AI-driven aerial and ground robots for pipeline and tank inspection.

Collaborative robots (cobots): Working alongside human operators for hazardous material handling.

24.5 Predictive Regulatory Compliance

AI models forecasting regulatory changes and suggesting adjustments to formulations or processes ahead of time.

Automatic cross-referencing of new safety and environmental standards with existing product lines.

Digital twins ensuring all changes meet compliance before plant implementation.

24.6 AI-Enhanced Supply Networks

Real-time coordination between suppliers, manufacturers, and distributors using multi-agent AI systems.

AI that automatically negotiates supply contracts based on market conditions, demand forecasts, and quality requirements.

Blockchain integration to guarantee traceability of raw materials and final products.

24.7 The Rise of Hybrid Human–AI Expertise

Chemical engineers and AI specialists will co-design processes.

Operators will shift from manual adjustments to strategic oversight of AI systems.

Training programs will focus on AI literacy alongside chemical engineering fundamentals.

24.8 Challenges Ahead

Data silos remain a major obstacle to AI scalability.

Ethical and safety concerns will intensify as AI autonomy grows.

Workforce reskilling will be essential to fully realize AI's benefits.

Chapter 25 – Conclusion

Artificial Intelligence is no longer a futuristic idea for the chemical industry — it is a practical, proven, and rapidly advancing tool that is reshaping how we research, design, produce, and deliver chemical products.

From accelerating R&D with generative AI to optimizing processes in real time, the technology is steadily moving from pilot projects to core business systems.

25.1 The Shift from Experimentation to Integration

In the early stages, AI was often tested in isolated use cases: a predictive maintenance model here, a quality control vision system there. Today, leading chemical companies are embedding AI into entire value chains — linking R&D, production, supply chain, and customer engagement in an integrated, data-driven framework. The competitive edge no longer comes from whether AI is used, but how deeply and effectively it is embedded.

25.2 Strategic Imperatives for the Industry

Invest in Data Infrastructure – AI's accuracy and usefulness depend on clean, complete, and accessible data.

Build AI Talent and Partnerships – Blend chemical engineering expertise with data science skills.

Focus on Business Outcomes – Every AI initiative should have a clear impact on productivity, cost, safety, or sustainability.

Manage Change Proactively – AI adoption is as much about people and culture as it is about algorithms.

25.3 The Human–AI Partnership

Despite the headlines about "autonomous plants," AI will not replace the human role in chemical manufacturing. Instead, it will shift the focus from manual, repetitive tasks to strategic decision-making and innovation. The most successful organizations will be those where humans and AI systems work together seamlessly, each doing what they do best.

25.4 Looking Ahead

The next decade will see:

Autonomous chemical plants capable of self-optimizing in real time.

Sustainable production driven by AI-enabled energy and waste reduction.

Faster materials innovation through generative design and simulation.

Connected global supply networks coordinated by AI agents.

These advancements will not come without challenges — from data security to ethical governance but the benefits will far outweigh the risks for those who move decisively.

25.5 Final Word

The chemical industry has always been an innovation leader — from the industrial revolution's early processes to the modern era of advanced materials.

AI is simply the next great tool in that tradition. Companies that start now, experiment boldly, and scale intelligently will define the future of chemicals.

The message is clear: AI in the chemical industry is not optional — it is the next stage of competitiveness, sustainability, and growth.

www.ingramcontent.com/pod-product-compliance
Lightning Source LLC
Chambersburg PA
CBHW050527240926
51846CB00003B/730
* 9 7 8 9 3 7 5 4 2 6 4 7 9 *